READ TO WORK

BUSINESS

PHYLLIS DUTWIN

CAMBRIDGE ADULT EDUCATION
A Division of Simon & Schuster
Upper Saddle River, New Jersey

Author: **Phyllis Dutwin**
Series Editorial Consultant: Harriet Diamond, *President, Diamond Associates,*
   Multifaceted Training and Development, Westfield NJ

Director, Editorial & Marketing, Adult Education: Diane Galen
Market Manager: Will Jarred
Assistant Market Manager: Donna Frasco
Editorial Development: Learning Unlimited, Inc.
Project Editors: Douglas Falk, Elena Petron
Editorial Assistants: Kathleen Kennedy, Derrell Bradford
Production Director: Kurt Scherwatzky
Production Editor: John Roberts
Art Direction: Pat Smythe, Kenny Beck
Cover Art: Jim Finlayson
Interior Design & Electronic Page Production: Levavi & Levavi
Photo Research: Jenifer Hixson

Photo Credits: p. 6: David Young-Wolff, Photo Edit; p. 14: Bob Daemmrich, Stock Boston; p. 22: Scott and Gillian Aldrich; p. 32: Rob Goldman, FPG; p. 40: Beryl Goldberg; p. 48: Michael Newman, Photo Edit; p. 58: Cindy Charles, Photo Edit; p. 66: Scott and Gillian Aldrich; p. 74: Bill Bachman, Photo Edit; p. 84: David Young-Wolff, Photo Edit; p. 92: Ron Rovtar, FPG; p. 100: Marleen Ferguson, Photo Edit

Printed in the United States of America
  3 4 5 6 7 8 9 10   01

ISBN: 0-8359-4677-0

CAMBRIDGE ADULT EDUCATION
A Division of Simon & Schuster
Upper Saddle River, New Jersey

CONTENTS

T O   T H E   L E A R N E R

Welcome to the *Read To Work* series. The books in this series were written with you, the adult learner, in mind. Good reading skills are important in the world of work for these reasons:

◆ They may help you get the job you want.
◆ They will help you learn how to do your job well.
◆ They can help you get a better job.

The lessons in this book, *Read To Work: Business,* will help you improve your reading skills. As you work through the lessons, you will also learn about jobs in office support, customer service, finance, and other areas of business.

UNITS

Read To Work: Business is divided into four units. Each unit covers different kinds of jobs. You can look at the **Contents** to see what fields and jobs are covered in this book.

LESSONS

Each unit contains at least 3 lessons. Each lesson teaches one reading skill and covers one kind of job. Here are some things to look for as you read each lesson:

Words to Know are words you will learn in the lessons. Look for the meaning of each new word to the left of what you are reading. You will also see a respelling of the words like this: *pronunciation* (proh-nun-see-AY-shuhn). This respelling will help you say the word correctly. There is a guide to help you with the respellings on page 105.

Job Focus describes the job in the lesson. It also tells you what types of skills are needed to do the job.

How It Works teaches you about the reading skill and how you can use it.

Readings include memos, pages from handbooks and manuals, posters, product guidelines, safety notices, and articles from company newsletters. If you look through this book, you will see that the reading passages look different from the rest of the lesson. They are examples of reading materials from the world of work.

Check Your Understanding questions can be multiple choice, short answer, or true/false. They will help you check that you understand the reading.

On the Job gives you a chance to read about real people as they do their jobs.

OTHER LEARNING AIDS

There are other learning aids at the back of the book. They are:

Respelling Guide: help with pronouncing words
Resources: where to get more information on the jobs in the book
Glossary: definitions of the Words to Know
Index: job names in the book
Answer Key: answers to *Check Your Understanding* and *Lesson Wrap-Up* questions

Now you are ready to begin using *Read To Work: Business*. We hope that you will enjoy this book and learn from it.

Jobs in Information Handling

Keeping a business running smoothly takes the work of many people. Handling information is especially important.

In this unit, you will read about three kinds of workers who handle information. Receptionists help manage the office telephone system. They also are the first people to talk to visitors. Mail clerks arrange for the delivery of mail and packages. Mail clerks decide the best way to send items. Messengers deliver special items that must be carried by hand to a customer or another business.

All these workers read work materials on the job. For example, they may read company manuals. They may read instructions on forms. Or they may read directions for making deliveries. Workers who handle information depend on their reading skills to do their jobs well.

This unit teaches the following reading skills:

- finding the main idea
- finding details that support the main idea
- following directions

You will learn how the workers who handle information use these reading skills in their work.

Working as a Receptionist

▼▼▼▼▼▼▼▼▼▼▼▼

Words to Know

clients

communicate

courteous

employees

firm

reschedule

transfer

update

A receptionist (rih-SEHP-shuhn-ihst) is one of the most important people in an office. This is because the receptionist is the first person to talk to visitors. A helpful receptionist makes visitors feel good about a company. This is good for business.

When visitors come to the office, they ask for different kinds of help. The receptionist must know how to give visitors the help they need. To make sure the receptionist knows what to do, the company may give the receptionist a manual (MAN-yoo-uhl). The manual is a book of instructions. It explains every part of the job. The receptionist must understand these instructions.

When you read material on the job, you need to understand what it is about. You begin your reading with this question: What is the most important idea in this material? When you do this, you are taking a very important step. You are **finding the main idea.** Often, the main idea is directly stated in the reading. The title may also give you a clue to finding the main idea.

Job Focus

Receptionists do many things. Two important tasks are greeting visitors and answering the telephone. The receptionist makes visitors and callers feel good about the company. This is the receptionist's most important task. Receptionists should be friendly and polite, have good telephone manners, and be able to use a computer.

About 904,000 people are working as receptionists. Many receptionist jobs should be available through the year 2005. That is because companies need good receptionists. Also, receptionists often move up to other jobs in their companies. This leaves openings for new receptionists.

Finding the Main Idea: How It Works

The main idea is the most important idea in a reading. The main idea sums up what the reading is about. The first step in **finding the main idea** is asking this question as you read: What is the most important idea in this reading?

The main idea of a reading is often stated in the first paragraph. But if the reading has a title, you have a clue to the main idea. The title tells the subject of the reading. The subject is a clue to what the reading is about.

Below is Chapter 2 of a company manual. Read the chapter. Ask yourself, "What is the most important idea?"

transfer (TRANZ-fer) switch a telephone call from one place to another

---

Chapter 2
TRANSFERRING TELEPHONE CALLS

To **transfer** calls quickly and correctly, follow these steps. First, tell the caller what you are doing. Be polite. Say, "Please wait a moment. I'm transferring your call." Next, press the transfer button on the phone. The button will light up. When it is lit, press the staff member's number. Wait for the staff member to answer. Say that a caller is on the line. Give the name of the caller. Then, hang up the phone.

Sometimes, staff members are away from their desks. If a staff member doesn't answer, follow these instructions. Offer to transfer the caller to voice mail. Explain that the caller can leave a message, which the staff member will listen to later. Press the transfer button. Then, press the staff member's voice mail number and hang up.

5

Reread the title. What is the subject of the chapter?

_____

The subject is *transferring telephone calls*. The title tells you the subject of the chapter.

Now, reread the first paragraph. Think about the subject. Then, underline the sentence that states the chapter's main idea.

The first sentence states the main idea. It says, *"To transfer calls quickly and correctly, follow these steps."* The main idea sums up the important information in the paragraph. It states that there are steps to follow when transferring calls.

What is the main idea of the second paragraph?

_____

The second sentence states the main idea. It is *"If a staff member doesn't answer, follow these instructions."*

Every paragraph in a reading has a main idea. Each of these main ideas supports the main idea of the whole reading.

Receptionists need to greet and welcome people who visit the office. Below is part of a receptionist manual. It explains how to greet people. Read the manual. Then, answer the questions that follow.

---

communicate
(kuh-MYOO-nuh-kayt) to share ideas or information with other people

clients (KLY-uhnts)
customers; people who do business with a company

courteous (KEHR-tee-uhs)
helpful and polite toward others

reschedule (REE-skehj-ool)
make another time for an appointment; make another plan

Receptionist Manual

Chapter 1:
Greeting Our Clients

You are a very important person in our company because you **communicate** with our **clients**. How you talk to them makes a difference. Usually, you are the first person from our company to greet a client. Our clients' opinion of us starts with you.

When a client comes to the office, be ready to do three things:

- ❖ greet the person
- ❖ find out the person's needs
- ❖ refer the person to the right staff member

In this way, you will help the client and serve our company well.

When you greet clients, pay attention to their needs. Make clients feel that they have your complete attention. Stop what you are doing. Look right at the client and smile. Say "hello," and ask how you can help. Then, help the client. Direct the client to the right staff member. Give the directions that the client needs. Always try to answer a client's questions clearly and completely.

Sometimes, our clients have to wait to see our staff. Be prepared for this by being **courteous**. Keep several kinds of magazines nearby. Offer clients coffee or tea. Be ready to show them how to use an outside telephone line. If we keep clients waiting, they may need to **reschedule** their day.

2   *Skills for Receptionists*

Answer each question based on the manual on page 4.

1. What is the main idea of the whole reading?

    a. Receptionists should have a good speaking voice.
    b. Receptionists' main task is to answer questions.
    c. How receptionists greet clients makes a difference in what clients think of the company.
    d. Receptionists should finish what they are doing before greeting clients.

2. What is the main idea of the second paragraph?

    a. The receptionist's job includes greeting, finding out needs, and referring.
    b. The receptionist's job includes typing and filing.
    c. The receptionist should be prepared to help clients use the telephone system.
    d. The receptionist's main task is answering questions.

3. What is the main idea of the third paragraph?

    a. Receptionists should give good directions.
    b. Receptionists should pay attention to clients' needs.
    c. Receptionists should smile and say "hello."
    d. Receptionists should offer to help clients with their work.

4. The main idea of paragraph 4 is that

    a. clients should not be kept waiting.
    b. receptionists should help clients plan their day.
    c. companies should offer magazines to clients.
    d. receptionists should be courteous toward clients.

5. How did the title of the reading help you find the main idea? Explain your answer.

Check your answers on page 115.

It was Anita's first day at Cambio & Oro. The office manager, Ruth, explained the receptionist's job. "It is one of the most important jobs in the law office," Ruth said. "You will be the first person to greet our clients. The way you do your job will tell clients a lot about us."

Anita had experience working with people. She had worked in a clothing store and as a cashier. But this was her first receptionist job. Anita wanted to do well.

Ruth gave Anita the company manual to read. Anita had never seen a manual before. At her other jobs, people just told her what to do. Anita thought that the manual was a great idea. She could reread it anytime. She would always know what to do. Ruth told her to ask about anything she didn't understand, especially the telephone system.

Here is something Anita read in the manual:

Putting Messages on Voice Mail

To connect a caller to a staff member's voice mail, do this:

- Press "transfer" and then 684.
- Wait to hear the greeting "Welcome to Cambio & Oro."
- Press the staff member's extension number.
- Hang up at once, and the caller can leave a message.

TALK ABOUT IT

1. Explain why reading is a necessary skill for Anita.

2. Describe the reading that Anita had to do. How will the manual help Anita on the job?

Receptionists may do different kinds of tasks. What receptionists do depends on where they work. Often, a receptionist in a law office keeps telephone records.

Lawyers make many calls to clients. Clients get charged for these calls. The receptionist keeps track of how much each call costs.

Sometimes, a law office hires a long-distance telephone service to help keep records. The memo and information sheet below are about this kind of service. Read the memo and information sheet. Then, answer the questions that follow.

M   E   M   O

Date: September 9
To: Charles Kaye, Receptionist
From: Albert Chue, Office Manager
Subject: C&D Telephone Systems

As you know, we need to keep records of our long-distance calls. We need to know which client was called and how much the call cost. This is done so that the **firm** will know whom to charge for the call.

C&D Telephone Systems will be helping us keep track of our long-distance calls. Here is an information sheet they sent us. Please read it carefully. The tasks of the receptionist are clearly explained. If you have any questions, please call me. I'll be happy to explain.

C&D Telephone Systems: Long-Distance Service

C&D uses a system of codes to organize long-distance service. The codes are made up of numbers. These numbers identify who is called. We will assign a code number to each of your clients. **Employees** also will have a code number.

The receptionist's tasks will be to
- write the code number on the client's folder
- enter the code number in a computer file
- give the client's code number to the employee serving him or her
- **update** the client code list monthly
- give the client code list to the staff

---

firm a business partnership of two or more people

employees (ehm-PLOI-eez) people who work for a company or business

update to give the latest news or information about a situation

Answer each question based on the memo and information sheet on page 7.

1. The main idea of the first paragraph of the memo is that the firm

   a. does not want its employees to make long-distance calls.
   b. has very high long-distance phone bills.
   c. wants its employees to make fewer phone calls.
   d. needs to keep records of its long-distance calls.

2. C&D Telephone Systems has been hired to

   a. teach the receptionist how to keep records of calls.
   b. repair the telephone system.
   c. help keep track of long-distance calls.
   d. keep all telephone records for the company.

3. C&D Telephone Systems will assign a code number to each

   a. receptionist.
   b. long-distance location.
   c. client and employee.
   d. office.

4. According to the memo, what does the company need to know about each long-distance call?

   a. how much the call cost and who was called
   b. who made the call and when it was made
   c. the client's name and telephone number
   d. the date and content of the call

5. Which of the following receptionist's tasks is *not* listed in the memo?

   a. Enter the code number in a computer file.
   b. Send the client a bill for all long-distance calls.
   c. Update the client code list monthly.
   d. Give the client code list to the staff.

6. The main idea of the information sheet from C&D Telephone Systems is that

Check your answers on page 115.

◆ LESSON WRAP-UP

The main idea is the most important idea in a reading. The main idea sums up what the reading is about. In longer readings, every paragraph has its own main idea. Each of these main ideas supports the main idea of the reading as a whole.

To find the main idea ask yourself, "What is the most important idea?" The answer to this question is the main idea. Another way is to look at the title of a reading. The title tells you the subject. And the subject is a clue to the main idea.

In this lesson, you have read parts of company manuals, memos, and instructions. In each case, you looked for main ideas. Finding main ideas helped you understand what you read.

I. Think about reading you do at home, at work, or in school. How will finding main ideas improve your reading?

Finish the sentence below.

Finding main ideas will help my reading by

2. Think about the reading you do on the job. The job may be one you have now, or it may be a job that you had in the past. What is the job? What did you read? Why was it important for you to understand the main idea of what you read on the job?

Write a paragraph based on the questions above.

Check your answers on page 115.

Handling Mail and Packages

Mail clerks do important work for companies. The mail clerk arranges for the delivery of the company's mail and packages. Mail clerks make sure that employees get all the mail and packages that come in for them. Mail clerks also help employees send mail and packages to other people.

Mail clerks must be careful to get mail to the right place. They also must decide the best way to send mail. To do so, mail clerks read charts, lists, and forms. They also read instructions. Mail clerks need good reading skills to do their job well.

All jobs involve details. Mail clerks need to know details like names and addresses. These details can change with each piece of mail delivered or package sent. So mail clerks must know how to look for details each time they read.

In this lesson, you will practice **finding details that support the main idea.** These important details explain the main idea. Sometimes, you can quickly find supporting details in a reading by looking for a list.

Job Focus

Mail clerks work in companies and in government. They sort and deliver incoming mail and packages. Mail clerks also handle mail that is sent out of the company. For that reason, mail clerks are sometimes called **shipping clerks.**

Mail clerks must be able to sort incoming mail quickly and correctly. Mail clerks also send a lot of mail. They need to know how to find the right delivery service and figure the costs.

Currently, there are about 130,000 mail clerk jobs. About 20 percent of these jobs are in the government.

Finding Supporting Details: How It Works

Everything that you read has a main idea and supporting details. **Supporting details** are specific facts and ideas. These facts and ideas support the main idea by telling more about it. Supporting details answer the questions *who? what? when? where? why?* and *how?*

The note below has many details. It was written by an office manager. The first sentence of the note states the main idea: Mail should be forwarded, or remailed, to the homes of employees who recently left the company.

As you read the note, look for details that support the main idea.

Mail Clerks:

Please forward the mail of employees who recently left the company. Their names and home addresses are listed below.

John Atherton
205 Federal Way
Boston, MA 02116

Max Fillmore
86 Park Plaza
Billerica, MA 01822

Tom Finnegan
One Newton Plaza
Boston, MA 02109

Renee Laval
100 Green Hill Drive
Salem, MA 01972

Which supporting details tell exactly *whom* the mail should be forwarded to?

The supporting details are *John Atherton, Max Fillmore, Tom Finnegan,* and *Renee Laval.* These specific names support the main idea by answering the question "Who?"

Which supporting details tell exactly *where* the mail should be delivered?

Did you choose the *home addresses in the list?* Then, you are right. Each of these supporting details answers the question "Where?"

Remember: Supporting details are specific facts or ideas. These facts and ideas support the main idea by telling more about it.

Mail clerks handle many different pieces of outgoing mail. When shipping items, mail clerks must think about costs. For example, they may decide to pay a higher cost to protect a valuable item. Then, if the mail service loses that item, it pays for the cost of replacing it.

Sometimes, mail clerks use special shipping services to send packages. These services use shipping forms. To complete these forms correctly, mail clerks read instructions. Read the shipping instructions below. Then, answer the questions that follow.

documents
(DAHK-yuh-muhnts) papers that contain important information; often, legal information

reference (REHF-uhr-uhns) **number** a number given to an item to track it from mailing to delivery

insure (ihn-SHOOR) to protect against loss

FLEET SYSTEMS: Shipping Instructions

Fleet Systems promises to deliver your packages and **documents** on time. You must give us the information that we need to do the job right. Please follow these instructions to complete the shipping form correctly.

Be sure to fill out all of the information. Include the name and telephone number of the person who will receive the package. You also should have a company **reference number** for each package. Note the number of packages. Remember to tell us how you want them sent. Then, sign the form. We also recommend that you **insure** any packages worth more than $100.

Below is a correctly completed form. Use it as a guide when you complete a form.

FLEET SYSTEMS Shipping Form	From Mario LaTella	Date December 5	Reference No. JJL29-015
Company Johnson, Johnson & LaTella	Dept/Flr: Suite 1200	Telephone (921) 555-5614	
Address 777 North Main Street Chicago, Il. 60202		Sender's Account #: 81277	

To Harris and Associates		Receiver's Name Pamela Harris	
Address 800 Riverside Drive Ocean Air, CA 95945		Telephone # (916) 555-0700	

Signature of Sender: **X Mario La Tella**

Total Number of Packages: 3   Value: $5,000.00

Service: (Choose One)

____ Same Day   ____ Overnight   ____ Second Day

____ International   ✓ Saturday Delivery

CHECK YOUR UNDERSTANDING

Answer the following questions based on the shipping instructions on page 12.

1. What is the main idea of the instructions?
   a. Fleet Systems promises on-time delivery, no matter what.
   b. It is important to follow Fleet Systems' instructions for filling out shipping forms.
   c. Fleet Systems will help mail clerks decide the best way to mail a package.

2. What is the main idea of paragraph 2?
   a. Include telephone numbers on the form.
   b. Check the spelling of all names on the form.
   c. Be sure to fill out all information on the form.

3. Which of the following details does *not* support the main idea of paragraph 2?
   a. Fleet Services will not deliver items worth more than $100.
   b. Every package should have its own reference number.
   c. It is important to note how many packages are to be sent.

Answer the following questions based on the shipping form on page 12.

4. Who is receiving the packages?

5. What is the receiver's work address?

6. When should the packages arrive?

7. If you were the mail clerk, would you insure the packages? Why or why not? Explain your answer.

Check your answers on page 115.

Vilma Albeno works for a firm called Accounting Associates. The firm has 50 accountants and 25 support staff.

Vilma is the firm's head mail clerk. She is responsible for all mail and packages that come in or go out of the office. Vilma likes the job. She has a lot of responsibility. She is in charge of two other mail clerks, Juan and Victor. They deliver incoming mail. They also take outgoing mail to the mail room. Vilma makes sure the mail goes out on time.

One thing surprised Vilma when she began working for Accounting Associates. Not all staff members want their mail delivered to them. Her boss, Sylvia, explained it this way: "The accountants get a lot of mail. Some mail, like ads, is unimportant. The accountants could never get their work done if they read all their mail. So each accountant's mail goes to an assistant. The assistant opens and sorts the mail. Then, the accountant looks at it."

"How do I know who gets what mail?" Vilma asked.

Sylvia explained, "I will give you a list of the accountants and the assistants who get their mail. Here is part of the list. Look at how it works. This will help you keep the details straight."

DELIVERING MAIL

Some assistants open mail for more than one person. When you deliver the mail, please do so in the following way:

Assistant	Opens Mail for These Accountants	Office #
Kris Roman	Paul Dinton, Kate Farrelli, William Smith	200
Paul Starr	Chris Dannon, Carol Sands, Charles Quinn	206
Lauri Vento	Suri Endo, Karen Berner, Martin Manning	301

TALK ABOUT IT

1. Describe two kinds of reading that Vilma does on the job.

2. Discuss why Vilma must know how to find supporting details when she reads.

Often, mail clerks use the services of the post office to send mail. The post office has many different kinds of services. Mail clerks must tell the post office which service they want to use.

To choose the right service, mail clerks read instructions and rate sheets like the ones below. Read the instructions and rate sheet. Then, answer the questions that follow.

express (ihk-SPREHS) special service that is faster than normal

---

Mail Clerks' Instruction Sheet

First-Class and **Express** Services

There are two main ways that we send letters—first class and express. Express is faster. But it also costs more. Use the express service only when a letter must arrive within one day. Mail all other letters first class.

Also be sure to weigh all letters, whether first class or express. Weight affects cost. The heavier the letter, the more it costs to mail.

The post office has given us a rate sheet to follow. Please use this sheet to figure the cost of sending each letter.

Rate Sheet

FIRST-CLASS RATES

Single Piece Weight (oz)	Rate
Not over 1	$0.32
Over 1 but not over 2	$0.55
Over 2 but not over 3	$0.78
Over 3 but not over 4	$1.01
Over 4 but not over 5	$1.24

EXPRESS-MAIL RATES

Weight (lbs)	Next Day *(item delivered to post office)*	Next Day *(item delivered to addressee)*
Less than 1	$10.25	$10.75
Not over 1	12.05	15.00
Not over 2	12.05	15.00
Not over 3	14.20	17.25
Not over 4	16.35	19.40

addressee (ad-rehs-EE) person to whom mail is sent

The following sentences are based on the first paragraph of the instruction sheet on page 15. Write **SD** on the line next to each supporting detail. Write **MI** on the line next to the main idea.

1. _____ Express service is faster than first-class service.

2. _____ Express service costs more than first-class service.

3. _____ Two mail services are first class and express.

4. _____ Use express service when a quick delivery is important.

The following sentences are based on the second paragraph of the instruction sheet. Write **SD** on the line next to each supporting detail. Write **MI** on the line next to the main idea.

5. _____ Be sure to weigh all letters.

6. _____ Heavier letters cost more to mail.

7. _____ Weight affects cost.

8. _____ Lighter letters cost less to mail.

Use the rate sheet on page 15 to answer the following questions.

9. A mail clerk finds that a first-class letter weighs $1\frac{1}{2}$ oz. How much postage should the clerk put on the letter?
   a. $0.32
   b. $0.55
   c. $0.78
   d. $10.50

10. On Monday morning, a mail clerk has to send a number of documents to a law firm. The documents must arrive by Tuesday. They weigh 3 pounds. How much will it cost to mail the documents?
   a. $0.78
   b. $1.01
   c. $14.20
   d. $17.25

Check your answers on page 115.

◆ LESSON WRAP-UP

To find supporting details, look for specific facts and ideas. Supporting details give more information about the main idea. They answer the questions *who? what? when? where? why?* and *how?*

Mail clerks handle many letters and packages. To do their jobs quickly and correctly, they must find the supporting details in lists and charts. They also must find the supporting details in instructions and on forms.

When you find supporting details, you understand more of what you read. You also remember more. Look for supporting details whenever you read materials at work. Your job will be easier to do—and you will do it better.

1. Think about the materials that you read at home, at work, and in school. Why is it important for you to be able to find the supporting details?
Finish the sentence below.

Finding the supporting details will help my reading because

2. Think about materials that you have read on the job. The job may be one that you have now, or it may be a job that you had in the past. What is the job? What did you read? Why was it important to find the supporting details when reading for the job?

Write a paragraph based on the questions above.

Check your answers on page 115.

Delivering Messages by Hand

Have you ever followed written directions to get from one place to another? Did you use a map to help you follow the directions? Messengers do these things every day on the job.

Messengers carry items from one business to another. The items may be letters or packages. Messengers deliver these items quickly and safely. In this way, they help businesses run smoothly.

In this lesson, you will learn how to follow the kinds of directions that messengers use. You will look at a map and written directions. You will read a memo with directions that tell where, when, to whom, and what to deliver. You will also read directions for safe driving. Though all these materials look different, you will use the same skill to understand them—**following directions.**

Job Focus

Messengers often work for businesses. Businesses use messengers for many reasons. One reason is fast service. Another reason is safety. A business may want a valuable item delivered by hand.

When a business needs a messenger and it doesn't have any of its own, it calls a messenger service. This special company sends messengers to pick up and deliver items.

Messengers must know the area in which they work very well. Messengers who drive vehicles must have a clean driving record.

There are about 133,000 people working as messengers. Many work for hospitals and medical offices. Others work for messenger services, banks, and other businesses.

Following Directions: How It Works

Everyone needs to follow directions on the job. These directions may be spoken or written. **Following directions** is especially important for messengers. They have to be at the right place at the right time. To do so, they read directions. They also look at maps and drawings. Maps and drawings can help them follow the directions.

When you read directions, follow these steps:

1. Ask yourself, "What is my goal?" Read the directions all the way through. Then, answer your question.

2. Get organized. Look for "clue words" like *first, then,* and *finally*. They tell you what order to follow.

3. Reread each part of the directions. Picture each step in your mind. A map or drawing can help you understand the steps.

Max is a messenger for Acme Messenger Service. He has to pick up and deliver a box of research papers. He can use the map below. Look at the map. Then, read the directions.

destination
(dehs-tuh-NAY-shuhn) place that one is going to; address one wishes to reach

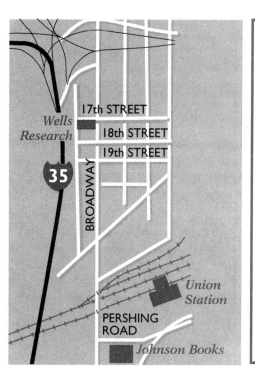

Destination: Johnson Books on Pershing Road
Pick up the box at Wells Research on Broadway at 17th Street. Then, go south to Pershing Road. Continue east on Pershing Road for one block. You will see Johnson Books on your right. Finally, go into the office, and deliver the box at the front desk.

What is Max's goal?

_____

Max's goal is to deliver a box to Johnson Books.

List two clue words that tell Max what order to follow.

___

You may have listed any two of these clue words: *then, continue, finally*. These words tell Max the order of the directions.

Often, messengers get written directions for each delivery. For example, Tom, a messenger, always receives a memo with detailed directions. Below is the memo that Tom received for his last pick-up and delivery. Read the memo. Then, answer the questions that follow.

SPEED-
COURIER SERVICE
WE DELIVER ON TIME!

September 11
To: Tom Courso
From: Jimmy Bright
Subject: Delivery to Law Offices of
Murray, Jones & Little
100 Robert Street, St. Paul

You will deliver documents to the office noted above. We will not have the papers until just before they have to be delivered. The papers must get to the lawyers on time. Please follow these directions.

First, note the law firm's new address. The firm has moved from Minneapolis to downtown St. Paul.

Pick up the documents to be delivered at Sage Studios on 15th Avenue. Drive two blocks to the Washington Avenue Bridge. After crossing the bridge, stay on Route 122 to Cedar Avenue. After you pass Cedar, look for the Route 35 E&W sign. Follow the 35 East sign. This will become Route 10.

Follow the "Downtown St. Paul" signs. Turn right onto University Avenue. Continue on University to Robert Street (Routes 12 & 52). Turn left onto Robert Street. The law offices are in the second building on the right.

When you arrive, give the documents to Gloria Abello. She is Ms. Murray's assistant. Then, call our office. We may have a pick-up for you in St. Paul.

Answer each question based on the memo on page 20.

1. Tom's goal is to deliver documents to

   a. a business in Minneapolis.
   b. an office on 15th Avenue.
   c. a law firm in St. Paul.

2. What is Tom's destination?

   a. 100 Robert Street
   b. the corner of Routes 12 and 52
   c. 35 East Cedar Avenue

3. The directions say that Tom should travel by

   a. bike.
   b. car.
   c. bus.

4. What should Tom do after he passes Cedar Avenue?

   a. drive two blocks to the Washington Avenue Bridge
   b. follow the "35 East" sign
   c. go west on Route 10

5. Which street will Tom be on *before* he turns onto Robert Street?

   a. Washington Avenue
   b. Cedar Avenue
   c. University Avenue

6. According to the directions, what should Tom do *last?*

   a. call the office for further instructions
   b. give the documents to Gloria Abello
   c. go to St. Paul for his next pick-up

Check your answers on page 116.

Jason has been searching the want ads to find a job. He passed the GED test a few months ago. Since then, he hasn't found a job that interests him. In fact, he wasn't even sure what kind of job to look for. Then, he and his friend Carlos had a talk.

"When I was looking for a job, my father asked me these questions and it really helped," Carlos said. "First, what do you like doing? Second, what are you good at?"

Jason thought for a few minutes. Then, he said, "You know, if I could, I would get in my car and travel. I love to drive, and I love to see new things. I'm a good driver, and I can find my way around the city easily. But how could I make money that way?"

Carlos said, "You've named something you really like to do. So why not look for a job that calls for driving? How good are you at reading maps? And following written directions?"

Jason answered, "Well, I've always been good at reading maps. What do you have in mind?"

"Have you thought about being a messenger?" Carlos asked. "That might be something you'd like doing. It's an important job, and you already have the skills you would need. You could get into the job market pretty quickly that way."

Jason thought about it for a little while and said, "You know, you might have a good idea. Let's see what messenger jobs are advertised in the newspaper."

TALK ABOUT IT

1. Describe the two things that Carlos thought Jason would have to read as a messenger.

2. Discuss why reading would be an important skill for a messenger.

Messenger services want their drivers to be safe. Often, they teach their drivers how to avoid accidents. The Acme Messenger Service teaches its messengers to drive safely by using training materials. Sometimes, the training materials have drawings. They can help the messengers understand the materials.

Read the safety training material below. Look at the drawing. Then, answer the questions that follow.

THE 2- TO 3-SECOND RULE

To avoid accidents, you need to keep a safe distance between you and the car in front of you. Use the 2- to 3-second rule for safely following other cars. This rule gives you time to brake to a stop when you see danger ahead. Here's how to follow the rule:

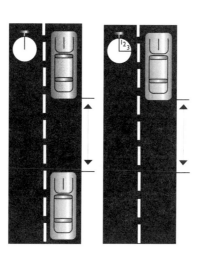

1. Choose a mark in the road. This can be a crack in the road or the beginning or end of a white line.
2. Begin to count as the car ahead of you passes the mark you have chosen.
3. Say, "1,001—1,002—1,003."
4. Be sure that you are able to say those three numbers before you pass the mark. This will mean that you are 2 to 3 seconds behind the car in front of you.

Remember that the 2- to 3-second rule works under certain **conditions.** Traffic should be normal. The weather should be good. Different conditions change the rules. Here are some examples:

- When following a large truck, increase the distance to 3 to 4 seconds.
- When on the highway, increase the distance to 4 to 5 seconds. You need the extra time to stop at higher speeds. For example, you need almost 5 seconds to stop at 60 miles per hour.
- When driving on bad roads or in bad weather, increase the distance to 6 seconds or more.

Follow the rules above to avoid **collisions.**

conditions (kuhn-DIHSH-uhnz) state in which a thing is

collisions (kuh-LIZH-uhnz) accidents in which two or more cars slide into each other

Answer each question based on the training material on page 23.

1. In the first paragraph of the training material, the messenger is told to

    a. change lanes often.
    b. never drive behind a big truck.
    c. drive slowly in bad weather.
    d. follow other cars at a safe distance.

2. Reread the second paragraph and its four steps. The first step directs the messenger to

    a. brake to a stop carefully.
    b. choose a mark in the road.
    c. count three cars as they pass.
    d. drive faster when there is traffic.

3. According to the training material, the driver should change to the 4- to 5-second rule when

    a. he or she is driving at higher speeds.
    b. there is a chance of rain.
    c. the driver is ahead of schedule.
    d. the road is dry and clear.

4. When driving behind a large truck, drivers should

    a. slow down at once.
    b. try to drive the same speed as the truck.
    c. be careful when the truck changes lanes.
    d. increase the following distance to 3 to 4 seconds.

5. When using the 2- to 3-second rule, the messenger should be able to say, "1,001—1,002—1,003" before

    a. passing the mark in the road.
    b. passing the car in front.
    c. driving one mile.
    d. changing lanes.

Check your answers on page 116.

◆ LESSON WRAP-UP

In this lesson, you learned a three-step plan for following directions:

1. Ask yourself, "What is my goal?" Read the directions all the way through. Then, answer your question.
2. Get organized. Look for "clue words" like *first, then,* and *finally.* They tell you what order to follow.
3. Reread each part of the directions. A map or drawing can help you understand the steps.

You also read different kinds of directions and practiced following them. You read directions in a note and in a memo. You looked at a map and drawing. And you read directions in training materials.

Use the skills you learned in this lesson whenever you need to follow directions. You will find that the work goes faster and is easier to do.

1. Think about the material that you read at home, at work, and in school. How will it help you to improve your reading if you can follow the directions?

Finish the sentence below.

Following directions will help my reading by

2. Think about the reading materials that you have on a job. The job may be one that you have now, or it may be a job you had in the past. What is the job? What did you read? Why was it important to follow directions in what you read on the job?

Write a paragraph based on the questions above.

Check your answers on page 116.

1. Write a sentence that explains how to find the main idea of a paragraph.

2. Why is it important to find supporting details when you read materials at work?

3. Explain how following directions can be an important skill in the workplace.

4. Think of the jobs that you learned about in this unit. Which job interests you the most? Why are you interested in this job? How could you learn more about it? Why would it be important to have good reading skills for this job?

Write a paragraph based on these questions.

Check your answers on page 116.

Unit Two

· Office Support Jobs ·

It takes many people to keep an office organized. Every office has records to file, schedules to keep, and information to share. The office support staff does this work.

In this unit, you will read about three types of office support workers. Secretaries help keep the office organized. They answer phones, keep files, type letters, and schedule appointments. Personnel clerks keep records about employees. Insurance processing clerks check facts on insurance forms. They share information about insurance with customers.

All these office support workers read work materials. They read memos, letters, and faxes. They check facts on forms. These employees need good reading skills to do their jobs well.

This unit teaches the following reading skills:

◆ making inferences
◆ comparing and contrasting
◆ drawing conclusions

You will learn how the office support workers use these reading skills in their work.

Working as a Secretary

Words to Know

correspondence

dictation

faxes

supplier

word processing

Memos, letters, reports, and minutes of meetings are different types of business materials. Memos may tell employees what to do on the job. Minutes are written records of what happened at a meeting. Reports explain what happened on a project.

Secretaries work with all of these types of materials. Sometimes, they take notes at meetings and write the minutes. They may type memos, letters, or reports for a boss. At other times, a boss may give a secretary some notes or ideas and ask the secretary to write the memo or letter.

To understand the materials that they work with, secretaries read for main ideas and supporting details. They also look for ideas that are suggested, rather than directly stated. When they read for ideas that are not directly stated, they are **making inferences** (IHN-fuhr-uhns-ehz).

Making inferences is an important reading skill for secretaries. Busy bosses expect their secretaries to be able to figure out some ideas on their own. In this lesson, you will practice making inferences as you read different types of business materials.

Job Focus

Secretaries help make sure that an office runs smoothly. They may answer the phone, keep files, type letters, and arrange meetings. What a secretary does depends on the business and the secretary's boss.

More than 3.3 million people work as secretaries in the United States. Many secretarial jobs are in the legal and medical fields. The number of secretarial jobs in these fields should grow through the year 2005. But many other fields also use secretaries. Secretaries work in retail, construction, banking, and real estate.

Making Inferences: How It Works

Making inferences is sometimes called "reading between the lines." Many ideas in a reading are directly stated. Other ideas are only suggested. When you make an inference, you figure out an unstated idea. To do this, you use information in the reading plus your own knowledge.

To make inferences, think about the directly stated ideas. They are clues to ideas that are only suggested. Use the clues and what you already know about a subject to make the inference.

Read the memo below.

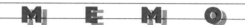

M E M O

November 1

To: All Staff
From: Elias Chari
Subject: Need for Another Secretary

Since Meredith left, it has been hard to get all our work done. We are now starting to look for another secretary. We want to ask for your help. You may know someone who is looking for a job. Let us know if you do.

Keep the following in mind before you suggest someone. Our new secretary will need to know how to use our computer system. He or she must also know how to take **dictation**. Even more important, the new secretary must enjoy working with all kinds of people. A big part of the job is working with others. We want to hire someone who knows how to get along—with us and our customers.

---

dictation (dihk-TAY-shuhn) material that is read aloud or recorded for a secretary so that he or she can type it

---

Which of the following is an inference based on the memo?
   a. Mr. Chari thinks that no one can take Meredith's place.
   b. Mr. Chari doesn't want the staff to help find a new secretary.
   c. Mr. Chari wants a secretary who is friendly and helpful.

The correct answer is *c. Mr. Chari wants a secretary who is friendly and helpful.* The main clues are "A big part of the job is working with others. We want to hire someone who knows how to get along—with us and our customers." Your own knowledge of what it means to be friendly also should help you pick answer *c*.

The other two choices are the opposite of what the memo suggests. Mr. Chari *is* looking for someone to take Meredith's place and *has* asked for help.

faxes (FAKS-ehz) written materials that are sent and received by machines over phone lines

Secretaries need to read many different types of materials. People communicate with businesses in different ways. They make phone calls, and send letters and faxes. **Faxes** are written materials that are sent and received over phone lines by fax machines. The letter or memo that is received is an exact copy of what the sender wrote.

Secretaries must read letters and faxes carefully in order to make important inferences. A secretary received the following fax from one of the company's best customers. Read the fax. Then, answer the questions that follow.

08–17   9:30   P. 01

Beautiful Blooms
F A X :

Tel: (206) 555-2311 Fax: 555-1123

DATE: August 17
TO: Complete Flower Supply
FROM: Will Evers, President
SUBJECT: Non-Blooming Spring Bulbs

You may remember how Beautiful Blooms became your customer. Our regular **supplier** did not deliver our spring order on time. The late order was costly for our business. So we decided to give your company a try.

Since then, I have been one of your larger customers of tulip bulbs. Every year for the past three years, I have bought at least 10,000 bulbs from you. I have always been happy with the flowers they produced. But this year, I am most unhappy. Over 50 percent of the bulbs failed to bloom.

I need to hear from you about this problem. Can you explain it? What can I expect you to do about our losses? Please reply at once.

supplier (suh-PLY-er) a company that sells goods that a business needs

Answer each question based on the fax on page 30.

1. Based on how the fax sounds, how does Will Evers feel?

    a. happy with the service he received
    b. thankful to the company for delivering on time
    c. upset about a problem with the bulbs
    d. angry and unwilling to speak with the supplier

2. From the first paragraph, you can make the inference that

    a. Mr. Evers understands that suppliers make mistakes sometimes.
    b. Mr. Evers may change suppliers if his company loses money.
    c. Complete Flower Supply always delivers on time.
    d. Complete Flower Supply has never made a mistake before.

3. From the second paragraph, what can you infer about the success of Beautiful Blooms this year?

    a. Beautiful Blooms is probably doing as well as it did last year.
    b. Beautiful Blooms will probably make more money than it did last year.
    c. Beautiful Blooms will probably go out of business.
    d. Beautiful Blooms may lose money on bulbs this year.

4. From the second paragraph, you can infer that Mr. Evers thinks that 50 percent of the bulbs failing to bloom is

    a. much too high.
    b. about right.
    c. a little high.
    d. somewhat low.

5. From the third paragraph, you can infer that Mr. Evers expects Complete Flower Supply to

    a. write a letter saying that they are sorry.
    b. deliver more flower bulbs.
    c. pay money to Beautiful Blooms to cover the losses.
    d. deliver much better bulbs next year.

Check your answers on page 116.

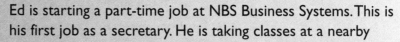

Ed is starting a part-time job at NBS Business Systems. This is his first job as a secretary. He is taking classes at a nearby community college. He especially likes his keyboarding (typing) and business English classes. Ed is learning how to write letters and memos. He also is learning how to communicate well over the phone.

Soon after his arrival on the first day, Vera, the office manager, came over to Ed to talk about the job.

She started by saying, "We're really glad you're working with us, Ed."

Ed answered, "Thank you. I'm looking forward to using the skills I've learned. Can you tell me more about my job?"

"I'd be happy to," Vera said. "First of all, you're sharing the 8-hour day with Mike—as you asked to do. You start work at 8:30 in the morning and you will leave at 1:00. Mike will be in at 12:30 and will stay until we close. You'll need to tell Mike what you've finished each day."

Ed said, "Yes, I've already talked to Mike. We've worked out a plan. We are going to keep a notebook in the desk and write down the tasks that we finish. That way, everyone will know what we're working on. I know that I'll be typing and handling Ms. Urso's mail. But what else will I be doing?"

Vera said, "When Ms. Urso is out of the office, you will need to pick up her phone messages and make sure she gets them as soon as she returns. You can keep a written record of who called, when, and the message."

TALK ABOUT IT

1. Think about what Ed might read during a day at the office. Describe the things that he might read.

2. What kinds of materials do you think Ed read to get ready for his new job?

word processing
(PRAH-sehs-ihng) typing and revising on the computer

correspondence
(kawr-uh-SPAHN-duhns) letters written or received

Secretaries have many tasks for which they use computers. For example, they can use **word processing** to enter **correspondence.**

The letter below was entered on the computer by the vice president's secretary. It is an answer to a customer's complaint. The letter tries to show the customer how important she is.

Read the letter. Think about what kinds of things the customer might infer about the company.

D & K FLOOR REPAIR

Darlene M. Kinney   December 20
34 Oak Ridge Drive
Los Angeles, CA 90019

Dear Ms. Kinney:

Thank you for telling us about the problem with our service call last month. We understand that you are unhappy with our work. We want to solve this problem for you.

Our records show that your regular service person, Larry, came to your home on November 22. He was to apply a Pacific Oak finish to your wood floors. Larry did not have enough of the finish with him. So he did not complete the job.

He told you that he would come back the next morning. Your letter says that he did not come back until November 24. You were not home. So he did not apply the rest of the finish at that time.

Ms. Kinney, we are sorry for any problems that we may have caused. The shipment of floor finish was late. It did not arrive at our business until the morning of November 24. Larry came to your house as soon as it arrived. But he should have called to explain.

We will send a team of workers to finish the work on your floors on the day of your choosing. There will be no charge for this work.

Again, we are very sorry about the mix-up. We will make every effort to be sure that this problem never happens again. Your business is important to us.

Sincerely,

Nita Graham

Nita Graham
Vice President of Customer Relations

Answer each question based on the letter on page 33.

1. Which of the following ideas can you infer from the first paragraph of the letter?

    a. The company wants to know when a customer is unhappy.

    b. The company does not think the customer is right.

    c. The company makes mistakes often.

    d. The company thinks the customer caused part of the problem.

2. You can infer that the customer was angry because

    a. the service person did not apply the finish in the right way.

    b. the company wanted to charge the customer to finish the job.

    c. the service person did not come on the day he said he would.

    d. the service person did not call to say he was sorry.

3. From the details in the letter, you can infer that Larry

    a. wanted to finish the job on November 24.

    b. forgot to call Ms. Kinney about the problem.

    c. has never made a mistake before.

    d. always works on Tuesdays.

4. One way Ms. Graham made the customer feel important was by

    a. blaming the problem on a late shipment of finish.

    b. explaining why Larry did not have enough finish.

    c. explaining how she would punish Larry for the mistake.

    d. offering to finish the job for no charge.

5. The letter says that D&K Floor Repair will make every effort to be sure that this problem never happens again. What is one thing the company could do to prevent the problem?

Check your answers on page 116.

◆ LESSON WRAP-UP

Not everything that you read gives you all the facts. In this lesson, you learned how to make inferences when you read. You learned to figure out unstated ideas. You put together clues in directly stated ideas and found the meaning behind them.

In this lesson, you learned to make inferences when reading business materials. You made inferences about ideas in a letter, a memo, and a fax.

Secretaries know that what they have learned before helps them to be better readers. They look at the facts they are given. They use what they know, and they see what is suggested. You, too, will get more out of your reading if you make inferences when you read.

I. Think about the material that you read at home, at work, and in school. How will it help you to improve your reading if you can make inferences?

Finish the sentence below.

Making inferences will help my reading by

2. Think about materials that you have read on a job. The job may be one that you have now, or it may be a job that you had in the past. What is the job? What did you read? Why was it important to be able to make inferences in what you read on the job?

Write a paragraph based on the questions above.

Check your answers on page 116.

Working in Personnel

▼▼▼▼▼▼▼▼▼▼▼

Words to Know

applicant

exceeds

Human Resources
Department

job application

performance reviews

prerequisites

punctuality

quality

quantity

supervisors

To succeed, companies must find and keep good employees. Personnel (puhr-suh-NEHL) clerks help companies meet this goal by keeping records. These records hold information about personnel, or the group of people employed by the company.

Personnel information is used to make important decisions. For example, it may be used to decide what people to hire. It also may be used to decide what training classes employees need.

To make decisions, personnel clerks **compare and contrast** personnel information. Often, the personnel information is on forms. They compare the information to see how it is the same. They contrast the information to see how it is different. Then, they report the results.

In this lesson, you will see how personnel clerks compare and contrast personnel information. You will read different forms that personnel clerks read. As you read, you will learn how comparing and contrasting is an important reading skill on the job.

Job Focus

Personnel clerks work in every kind of business. They work in banks, hospitals, and department stores. They also work in many government offices. Wherever they work, personnel clerks gather and keep information about employees. When others in the company need the information, personnel clerks get it for them. Personnel clerks should be very organized in their work. They need to pay careful attention to details.

About 123,000 people work as personnel clerks. From now until 2005, there will be job openings as clerks move up to other personnel jobs.

Comparing and Contrasting: How It Works

When you compare things, you see how they are the same. When you contrast things, you see how they are different. **Comparing and contrasting** can help you gather information to make decisions.

Suppose that you need to buy a pair of shoes. As you compare two pairs, you see the things they have in common. Both pairs look good and cost $25. But as you contrast the two pairs, you find an important difference. The second pair hurts your feet. Based on this information, you decide to buy the first pair of shoes.

Personnel clerks also compare and contrast information. They may compare and contrast information to decide what people to hire. This information may be on more than one form.

People who are looking for a job usually fill out a special form called a **job application.** Below are parts of two job applications. As you read them, practice comparing and contrasting.

job application
(ap-lih-KAY-shuhn) form that a person fills out when looking for a job at a company

Application for Employment at ABC Corporation
Name of **Applicant**: Mark Gordon
High School Diploma: ☒ yes ☐ no
Name/Address of School:
Parker High, Villa, IL 60126
College Degree:
None
Name/Address of College:
What job are you applying for? Sales Clerk

Application for Employment at ABC Corporation
Name of **Applicant**: Risa Beryl
High School Diploma: ☒ yes ☐ no
Name/Address of School:
Harris High, Lakes, CA 90035
College Degree:
Associate's Degree in Retailing
Name/Address of College:
Lakes Community College, Lakes, CA 90035
What job are you applying for? Sales Clerk

applicant (AP-lih-kuhnt) person who applies for something, such as a job

Compare the two applicants. In what ways are they the same? In what way are the applicants different?

_____

_____

You are correct if you wrote the following: *Both graduated from high school. Both are applying for the job of sales clerk.*

Risa Beryl has more education than Mark Gordon. She has an associate's degree in retailing.

By comparing and contrasting the applicants, the personnel clerk can gather information. The information helps the clerk decide which applicant might be better for the job. For example, Risa Beryl might be better because she has retail training.

Human Resources
(HYOO-muhn REE-sawrs-ehz)
Department part of a
company that sets rules for
hiring and firing, keeps
personnel records, and is in
charge of training and
benefits such as health
insurance

Sometimes, personnel clerks work in a **Human Resources Department** (HRD). This department is in charge of employee training. Personnel clerks in HRD may help employees figure out what training courses they need to take. Personnel clerks may also keep records of the courses that employees finish.

Read the course descriptions below. Then, answer the questions that follow.

supervisors
(SOO-per-veye-zuhrz) people
who direct the work of
others

prerequisites
(pree-REHK-wuh-zihts)
courses that must be taken
earlier

ACE COMPANY TRAINING
Manual of Courses

Course: SFTY 100

Safety Training for **Supervisors**— Learning to Look for Problems

Trained By: ACE Supervisor (already trained in SFTY 100)
Length: Four two-hour sessions   *Audience:* Supervisors
Prerequisites: None
Description: Instruction in basic safety rules and how to keep others safe on the job
Instruction Method: Classroom, video tapes, field tests
Supplied Materials: Seven self-study workbooks; observation checklists

Course: SFTY 102

Safety Training for Employees

Trained By: ACE employee trained as a trainer
Length: Four hours   *Audience:* ACE employees
Prerequisites: None
Description: Instruction in basic rules of safety
Instruction Method: Classroom, video tapes, role-playing
Supplied Materials: Four self-study workbooks

Answer each question based on the course descriptions on page 38.

1. Both courses are about the subject of

   a. supervising employees.
   b. working in personnel.
   c. learning to look for problems.
   d. safety training.

2. Which of the following supplies is used in both courses?

   a. observation checklists
   b. field tests
   c. self-study workbooks
   d. the basic rules of safety

3. Compare and contrast the length of the courses. Which is a true statement?

   a. SFTY 100 takes more time than SFTY 102.
   b. Both SFTY 100 and SFTY 102 are the same length.
   c. SFTY 102 takes twice as long as SFTY 100.
   d. Both courses take four sessions to complete.

4. For both courses, the training is done by

   a. an ACE supervisor.
   b. someone who works for ACE.
   c. a Human Resources Department employee.
   d. a teacher from a local college.

5. In order for someone to take course SFTY 102, he or she must

   a. take SFTY 100.
   b. be a supervisor.
   c. be trained as a trainer.
   d. be an ACE employee.

6. Contrast the titles and descriptions of the courses. Write a brief paragraph explaining how what is taught in the courses may be different.

Check your answers on page 117.

Christina works in the Human Resources Department (HRD) of the Sharp Machine Company. Christina is a personnel clerk. She keeps many important records about the people who work at Sharp. Her boss, Donna, is the head of the department.

Every Friday morning, Christina checks the weekly attendance reports. They tell how many employees in each department were absent.

Last spring, Sharp began having worker attendance problems. Many workers were taking days off. The supervisors have been working to solve this problem. They have asked HRD to see if attendance has improved.

Christina reads a memo from Donna. The memo asks for attendance numbers for the past three months. Christina looks up the numbers. She compares and contrasts the numbers for June, July, and August. She is glad to see that attendance is getting better.

Christina types a short memo stating the numbers as well as an idea she has. Later, Donna asks to see her.

"After looking at the attendance at Sharp," Donna said, "I'm really happy with what I see. I want our employees to know that we have noticed the improvement. I like your idea to give awards for good attendance. Maybe we could have a company meeting to give out the awards."

Christina said, "I think that's a great idea! I'll check the calendar. I'll find a good date for the meeting. Then, you can see if the date is OK with the supervisors. I'll also find the employee with the best attendance in each department. I can figure out which department has the best attendance, too."

"Let me know what you find," Donna replied.

TALK ABOUT IT

1. Describe two things that Christina reads as a part of her job.

2. How do reading skills help Christina to do her job?

LESSON 5 ◆ WORKING IN PERSONNEL

performance
(per-FAWRM-ans) **reviews**
ratings of how well or
poorly people do their work

quality (KWAHL-uh-tee)
level of excellence

quantity (KWAHN-tih-tee)
amount

exceeds (ehk-SEEDZ) goes
beyond

punctuality (punk-choo-AL-
ih-tee) being on time

Sometimes, personnel clerks work with personnel information from supervisors. The supervisors do **performance reviews** in which they rate the work that employees do. Then, the personnel clerk files the review in the personnel record. When someone in the company needs the information, the clerk looks it up. For example, suppose that an employee wants to work in a different department. The supervisor of that department might call to see if the employee is a good worker.

In a performance review, work is often rated on forms like the ones below. Read the forms. Then, answer the questions that follow.

Employee Job **Performance**

Name: _Stuart Lee_   Date: _10/5_

I. Quality of Work
How often does the worker make errors?

I	[2]	3
Often	Once in a while	Seldom

Comments: _Stuart makes errors when_
he works too fast.

II. Quantity of Work
How well does the worker meet department goals for work completed?

I	2	[3]
Below goals	Meets goals	**Exceeds** goals

Comments: _Stuart finishes his work_
each day.

III. Attendance/Punctuality
How often is the worker absent or late?

[1]	2	3
Often	Once in a while	Seldom

Comments: _Stuart is late too often._

IV. Use of Work Time
How well does the worker use his/her time?

I	2	[3]
Poorly	Fair	Well

Comments: _Stuart works quickly and_
stays on task.

Total Score: _9_

Employee Job Performance

Name: _Annie Kim_   Date: _7/3_

I. Quality of Work
How often does the worker make errors?

I	2	[3]
Often	Once in a while	Seldom

Comments: _Annie's work is excellent._

II. Quantity of Work
How well does the worker meet department goals for work completed?

I	[2]	3
Below goals	Meets goals	Exceeds goals

Comments: _Annie could work faster to_
get more done.

III. Attendance/Punctuality
How often is the worker absent or late?

I	2	[3]
Often	Once in a while	Seldom

Comments: _Annie is rarely absent or late._

IV. Use of Work Time
How well does the worker use his/her time?

I	2	[3]
Poorly	Fair	Well

Comments: _Annie works hard the_
entire day.

Total Score: _11_

Answer each question based on the forms on page 41.

1. Compare and contrast the ratings on Stuart Lee's job performance form. What did Stuart score lowest in?

    a. Quality of Work
    b. Quantity of Work
    c. Attendance/Punctuality
    d. Use of Work Time

2. Read the comments on Annie's job performance form. Something Annie could do to improve is

    a. do a higher quality of work.
    b. work faster.
    c. be on time.
    d. work hard all day.

3. By looking at "Quantity of Work," the reader can tell whether workers

    a. meet department goals for the work they do.
    b. do their jobs neatly.
    c. make many errors when they work.
    d. miss work too often.

4. Compare and contrast the two job performance forms. Which is a true statement?

    a. Both workers seldom make errors.
    b. Both workers are late for work too often.
    c. Stuart Lee has a higher total score than Annie Kim.
    d. Both workers make good use of their work time.

5. An employee who works fast but makes many mistakes would probably score low in

    a. Quality of Work.
    b. Quantity of Work.
    c. Attendance/Punctuality.
    d. Use of Work Time.

6. If you were a supervisor who needed a new employee, which worker would you hire? Why?

Check your answers on page 117.

◆ LESSON WRAP-UP

In this lesson, you learned how to compare and contrast as you read. When you looked to see how information was the same, you practiced comparing. When you looked to see how information was different, you practiced contrasting. Comparing and contrasting can help you gather information to make decisions.

Comparing and contrasting is an important skill for personnel clerks. These clerks have to answer questions for other employees. For example, supervisors depend on personnel clerks to give them correct information about workers. Supervisors may need information about how well workers do their jobs. Personnel clerks compare and contrast information in personnel records to get the answers.

1. Think about the material that you read at home, at work, and in school. How will it help you to improve your reading if you know how to compare and contrast information?

Finish the sentence below.

Being able to compare and contrast will help my reading by

2. Think about the materials that you have read on a job. The job may be one that you have now, or it may be a job that you had in the past. What is the job? What did you read? Why was it important to be able to compare and contrast as you read the material?

Write a paragraph based on the questions above.

Check your answers on page 117.

Checking Insurance Forms

There are many different kinds of insurance (ihn-SHOOR-uhns). People may have health, life, and car insurance. Home owners buy insurance to pay for losses from fires, floods, or other disasters. Workers have insurance that pays them if they are hurt on the job. Businesses have insurance to pay for losses due to property damage.

When something goes wrong, the person or business can put in a claim, or request for payment. Often, the claim is made by filling out a form. An insurance processing (PRAH-sehs-ihng) clerk then takes steps to see that the claim is properly handled, or processed.

Sometimes, people make incorrect claims. Insurance processing clerks must make judgments about whether claims are correct. To make a good judgment, clerks **draw conclusions** based on facts they are given and facts they already know. This skill protects both the person and the insurance company.

In this lesson, you will read claim forms and other kinds of materials that insurance processing clerks read. As you read, you will practice drawing conclusions.

Job Focus

Insurance processing clerks must be good with details. They must check claim forms and other paperwork to see that information is correct. They must know about the kinds of insurance their company sells. Insurance processing clerks also need good "people skills." They talk to customers to get information and answer questions. Good computer skills are important, too.

About 133,600 people work as insurance processing clerks. The number of jobs is expected to grow. Workers with computer skills have a better chance of getting a job in this field.

Drawing Conclusions: How It Works

Drawing conclusions means making judgments or decisions based on facts. To draw a conclusion, you use the facts that you are given and the facts you already know.

Here are a few steps you can use to draw conclusions. In step 1, figure out what information you have learned from the reading. In step 2, answer the question, "What do I already know about this topic?" In step 3, see if you can form a judgment or decision about what you have read. Your judgment or decision will be based on steps 1 and 2.

Insurance processing clerks must be good at drawing conclusions. Clerks talk to customers and answer questions about insurance policies (PAHL-uh-seez). The policy is a written agreement between the customer and the insurance company. The policy explains what losses the insurance will—and will not—cover, or pay for.

Below is part of an insurance policy for a business. Read the policy.

coverage (KUV-er-ij) losses that an insurance company will pay for

---

BCH, Inc. Policy

Limits on **Coverage**

1. **Cause of Damage.** This policy does not cover damage caused by misuse of office equipment, insects, or normal wear and tear.
2. **Location of Office.** This policy does not cover damage to a business that is run out of a home.
3. **Office Coverage Only.** This policy covers only the office where the business is located, not the entire building.
4. **Inspection Required.** This policy will not start until BCH can walk through and fully inspect, or check, the office.

A friend of yours is starting a business. You know that your friend will be running the business out of his home. Review the policy. Would the policy be a good choice for your friend? Why?

_____

If you said *No,* you drew a correct conclusion. *The policy is a bad choice because it does not cover home businesses.* To draw this conclusion, you looked at the information in the policy. You recalled what you already knew about your friend's business. Then, you made a judgment, or decision.

Insurance processing clerks answer customers' questions about policies. The clerks use computers to **access** the information customers want.

Usually, people want to know about the coverage they have. They want to know if certain losses are covered by their policies.

Part of an insurance policy is shown below. Read the policy. Then, answer the questions that follow.

Business Owner's Coverage

Water and Fire Damage

■ **Repair Costs**

If loss or damage occurs because of water and/or fire, we will pay the cost of replacement. That means, we will pay to tear out and replace the damaged part of the building. We will not pay the cost of repairing the problem that caused the damage.

■ **Loss of Income**

During the repair period, we will pay for loss of business income from the date of the damage through the time it takes to make repairs. This period of time is limited to no more than 12 months in a row.

Losses that can be claimed are limited to the **net income** that your business would have earned during the time period.

■ **Operating Expenses**

During the repair period, we will pay the usual costs of doing business. These operating expenses include the cost of normal business operations and payroll. Your coverage is limited to the time it takes to make all repairs (no more than 12 months from the date of the damage).

■ **Extra Expenses**

If you choose to move your business to a new location during the repairs, we will pay for extra expenses that come from moving.

Covered extra expenses include:
1. the cost of moving to a new work place
2. the cost of renting equipment for the new location

Answer each question based on the policy on page 46.

1. A restroom is right above an office covered by the policy. During the night, a sink overflows. In the office, the water causes damage to a wall and the ceiling. After reading the policy, you can conclude that the insurance company will

    a. pay to repaint the ceiling only.
    b. pay nothing on this claim.
    c. refuse to repair or replace the sink.
    d. cancel the business's insurance policy.

2. A company wants to move its office to a new location while the old one is being repaired. Based on the policy, you can conclude that the insurance company will cover the cost of

    a. renting business machines for the new office.
    b. buying new furniture for the new office.
    c. painting the new office.
    d. hiring a new office manager.

3. A business covered by this policy is closed because of fire damage. The business moves to a new office building. The repairs may take up to two years to make. Based on the facts in the policy, you can conclude that the policy will pay for

    a. the loss of business income for the two-year period.
    b. all the company's operating expenses until the repairs are completed.
    c. the cost of repairing the problem that started the fire.
    d. the loss of business income, operating costs, and extra expenses for the first 12 months.

4. In each section of the policy, the insurance company places a limit on how much it will cover. What conclusion can you draw about the reason for the limits?

Check your answers on page 117.

Elena began work at Southeast Insurance Company three weeks ago. She has been training as an insurance processing clerk for two weeks. Last week, she worked with someone at her side. Now, she is ready to work on her own.

During her training, Elena learned that she would handle many details. She would start files for new customers. She would also call customers for information they left out of forms. Elena also would add or change information in files.

Elena's earlier computer training was very helpful. She learned how to use the company's software during her two weeks of training. Almost all of her work would be done on the computer.

When a customer calls, Elena accesses information on the computer. Then, she does whatever is needed. Her boss, Mr. Jordan, said that she would get lots of change of address calls.

He also said, "You will get phone calls from people who want you to tell them exactly what their insurance policy covers. Until you receive more training about our policies, you are not ready to give answers about claims. Listen to their questions. Then, decide who would be the best person for the customer to talk to. Usually, you will give the call to a person who handles claims."

Elena wanted to know how she could know to whom to give the call.

"Use your directory," Mr. Jordan answered. "That gives you the names of all the employees and their job titles."

As Elena thought about her talk with Mr. Jordan, she heard her telephone ringing. She picked up the phone and said, "Hello. This is Elena. How may I help you?"

TALK ABOUT IT

1. Describe two things that Elena will read in this job.

2. Why is it important for Elena to know how to draw conclusions on the job?

When workers are hurt in an accident on the job, they can make a claim for **workers' compensation.** Once claims are made, insurance processing clerks make sure that all the paperwork is done. An important form that must be filled out is called "Employer's First Report of Injury." This form contains detailed information about the worker's injury. By reading the form, the insurance processing clerk can draw conclusions about the accident.

Read the form below. Then, answer the questions that follow.

EMPLOYER'S FIRST REPORT OF INJURY

State of Utah, Department of Labor
Division of Workers' Compensation

Employee Information
Soc. Sec. No. 509-06-0555 [M] F
Name Craig Worth
Address 302 Ogden Dr.
City/State/Zip Orem, UT
84057
Phone (801) 555-2924
Date of Birth 09/20/55
Job Title Driver   Date employed 10/25/94

Employer Information
Insurance No. 315-AC-49
Name XYZ Business Paper
Address 109 E. 300 N.
City/State/Zip Provo, UT
84601
Phone (801) 555-1001 Ext. 59
Type of Business Paper Supplier

Injury Information
Injury Date 08/11/98
Place where injury occurred: ABJ Printing, 1308 Apple Lane, Provo, UT 84604, curbside near back entrance to company
Time workday began 10:15 A.M.   Time of injury 5:25 P.M.
Date employer notified 08/13/98
Has employee returned to work? No
Injury occurred on company property? No
Describe how the injury happened. Driver was using the truck lift to lower cartons of paper to the street level. According to the driver, the lift locked up and the cartons fell toward him. He injured his left leg.

Medical Information
Where treated Utah County Hospital
Address Provo, UT 84601
Kate Roberts
Employer's Signature

Witness Information
Name (None)

Address
8/15/98
Date

Answer each question based on the form on page 49.

1. From the title and information in the form, you can conclude that this form is filled out by

    a. the employee who was injured.
    b. the employer.
    c. the hospital or doctor.
    d. a witness to the accident.

2. From the dates shown on the form, you can conclude that

    a. Craig Worth was a new employee of XYZ Business Paper.
    b. the employer, Kate Roberts, wants to be told immediately when an accident happens.
    c. Craig Worth has been working for XYZ Business Paper for nearly four years.
    d. the employer was unhappy with the quality of the employee's work.

3. Which of these facts must be known about the injured employee in order to fill out the form?

    a. the driver's license number of the employee
    b. the employee's date of birth
    c. the employee's level of education
    d. the name of the employee's doctor

4. Which of the following statements can you conclude about the accident?

    a. The problem with the lift had happened before.
    b. The employer was there when the accident happened.
    c. The employer thinks the accident was the driver's fault.
    d. The driver was alone at the time of the accident.

5. The form states that the employee has not returned to work. What reason might explain why the employee has not returned to work? Draw a conclusion from the information given on the form.

Check your answers on page 117.

◆ LESSON WRAP-UP

In this lesson, you learned to draw conclusions as you read. To draw conclusions, you gathered information from forms and policies. You recalled what you already know. Then, you made a judgment, or decision.

Insurance policies and claim forms are not easy reading. They contain many pieces of information. Insurance processing clerks use the information to make decisions. They might draw conclusions about what is covered by insurance companies. Or, they might draw conclusions about a claim. To do their job well, they need to draw good conclusions based on what they read and what they already know.

1. Think about the material that you read at home, at work, and in school. How will drawing conclusions as you read improve your understanding?

Finish the sentence below.

Drawing conclusions as I read will help my understanding because

2. Think about the reading materials that you have read on a job. The job may be one that you have now, or it may be a job that you had in the past. What is the job? What did you read? Why was it important to be able to draw conclusions from the information you read on the job?

Write a paragraph based on the questions above.

Check your answers on page 117.

◆ UNIT TWO REVIEW

1. Write a definition of *making inferences*. Give an example that explains your definition.

2. When you compare and contrast the details in a reading, what are you trying to find out?

3. You are looking for someone to hire for a certain job. You know the skills that are needed for the job. You also have job applications that list people's past jobs and duties. Explain how you can use the skill of drawing conclusions to fill the job opening.

4. Think of the jobs that you learned about in this unit. Which job interests you the most? Why are you interested in this job? How could you learn more about it? Why would it be important to have good reading skills for this job?

Write a paragraph based on these questions.

Check your answers on page 118.

Unit Three

• Jobs in Customer Service •

Most businesses make money by selling things to customers. Workers must be able to find out what the customers need and then do their best to meet those needs.

In this unit, you will read about three kinds of workers who help customers directly. Order clerks take orders from customers. They write the orders carefully to make sure that the customers get the items they want. Auto club assistants help customers read and understand maps to plan trips. Customer service representatives handle complaints, solve problems, and work hard to make sure that customers are happy.

All these employees read on the job. Order clerks read forms and catalog information. Auto club assistants read maps and travel guides. Customer service representatives read forms, letters from customers, and office memos.

This unit teaches the following reading skills:

- ♦ classifying information
- ♦ understanding visual information
- ♦ distinguishing fact from opinion

You will learn how workers in customer service use these reading skills in their work.

Taking Customers' Orders

Many people like to shop through catalogs. These booklets describe clothing, gifts, and other items for sale. When customers see something they want, they order it over the phone or through the mail. The item is then shipped to them. Whether a customer orders clothes, car parts, or office supplies, the order first goes to an order clerk. If a customer wants to buy clothing, an order clerk asks about size, color, and number of items. The clerk puts this information on an order form.

Order forms need a lot of detailed information. When clerks take an order, they have to find where to put each detail. On order forms, similar information is grouped together. **Classifying information** in this way makes the information easier to find.

In this lesson, you will read different order forms that order clerks read. One order form is for individual customers, or "home shoppers." Another order form is for business customers. On both forms, information is classified so that it is easier to read and understand.

Job Focus

Order clerks may work for stores or for catalog companies. Many order clerks take orders over the phone. Order clerks may also work with orders sent by mail or by fax.

Some order clerks take in-house orders. These are orders from co-workers. Large companies may keep parts in storage. When workers need parts, they call or fax their order to the company's order clerks.

There are about 310,000 people working as order clerks. Order clerks will be in demand through 2005.

Classifying Information: How It Works

Classifying means "putting similar items together in groups." To make items easy to find, stores classify the items. For example, shoes and socks have something in common. Both are worn on the feet. So stores put these items in the same area. They also give the area a name: "Footwear." In the same way, information on order forms is grouped under a heading, or title. The heading tells what the information has in common. **Classifying information** by grouping it under a heading makes it easier to read and understand.

To order items by mail, customers use order forms like the one below. Read the customer order form.

Housewares, Inc.

Shipping Information:

❏ Regular Mail
(allow 10 days to
2 weeks)

❏ Ground Shipment
(allow 4–5 days)

❏ Express Delivery
(2 business days)

Ordered by:

Name _____
Address _____
City, State, Zip _____
Telephone Number _____

Ship to: (If different from "Ordered by," include name and address below)

Name _____
Address _____
City, State, Zip _____
Telephone Number _____

Items:

Description	Quantity	Price Per Item	Total
_____	_____	_____	_____
_____	_____	_____	_____
_____	_____	_____	_____
_____	_____	_____	_____

One part of the form is in a box. What does the information in the box have in common?

_____

All the information in the box is about shipping. Notice that the box has a heading: "Shipping Information." This heading tells you what the information has in common.

Look at the order form again. There are two parts for addresses. What are the two parts? Why are both needed?

_____

_____

The two parts to the address are *(1) the person who ordered the item and (2) the person who will receive it. They may not be at the same address. A customer might order the item for someone else. So both parts are needed.*

Grand Clothing Company makes work clothes. Several times a year, the company sends a catalog to individual customers. Inside each catalog is an order form. To buy an item, customers fill out the order form. Then, they mail or fax it to the company.

When the order form arrives, an order clerk reads it. The clerk checks to see that the order form is complete.

Read the customer order form below. Then, answer the questions that follow.

unit price one part of the cost; the cost for one piece

expiration (ehk-spuh-RAY-shun) **date** the date after which something can no longer be used

---

Grand Clothing Company

32nd Street • Grand Rapids, MI 49513

3 STEPS TO EASY ORDERING:

Step 1

BILL TO:	SHIP TO:
Name_____	Name_____
Address_____	Address_____
Telephone_____	Telephone_____

Step 2

Catalog Item #	Description	Size	Quantity	**Unit Price**	Total

SUBTOTAL OF ALL ITEMS

Sales Tax (on subtotal) in NY and VA only	
Shipping and handling charges (from below)	
ORDER TOTAL	

Step 3

_____Check enclosed: Make payable to **Grand Clothing Company**

Please charge to my: _____ VIZA _____ MajorCard

_____ National Express _____ Explorer

If using a charge card, include card number, **expiration date**, and signature.

Card Number _____ Expiration Date _____

Signature _____

Shipping and Handling Charges

Up to $20	$4.75	$101.01 to $150	$14.98
$20.01 to $30	$5.75	Over $150	$15.98
$30.01 to $40	$6.98	**Additional Charges**	
$40.01 to $50	$7.98	Express Delivery	$7.50
$50.01 to $75	$10.98	Shipping To	
$75.01 to $100	$12.98	Another Address	$3.50

LESSON 7 ◆ TAKING CUSTOMERS' ORDERS

Answer each question based on the customer order form on page 56.

1. What would be the best heading for Step 1 of the order form?

    a. Method of Payment
    b. Ordered By/Ship To
    c. Item Information and Cost
    d. Reason for Ordering

2. A good heading for Step 2 of the order form is

    a. Tax and Shipping Information.
    b. Color and Number.
    c. Item Information and Cost.
    d. Customer Name and Address.

3. The best heading for Step 3 of the order form is

    a. Method of Payment.
    b. Charge Card Information.
    c. Mailing Checks.
    d. Sign on the Line.

4. A customer wants her order sent to a different address. How much extra does it cost to do this?

    a. $3.50
    b. $4.75
    c. $7.50
    d. It depends on the total of the order.

5. A customer wants to charge the mail order but forgets to write down the charge card number. What do you think the order clerk will do? Which step of the order form—1, 2, or 3—would be helpful to the order clerk? Why?

6. A customer spent $40.75 on clothes from Grand Clothing Company. How much will it cost to send the clothes to the customer's address? Which part of the order form would the order clerk read to find the answer?

Check your answers on page 118.

Angela is training Martin to be an order clerk for Gifts-By-Mail, Inc. Christmas is coming, and the company is extra busy. So it has hired Martin for the holiday season.

Angela explains that the company mails catalogs to customers. Each catalog has an order form. Most customers phone in their orders. They will tell Martin what they want, and Martin will fill out the order form on his computer. He will type in the right information.

Martin has a question. "How do you know what the customer's order form looks like?"

Angela smiles. "We have the same order form in our computers. We see on the computer screen exactly what the customer is looking at. We have other information, too. Our computers keep track of what we have in stock. When an item is in stock, it means that the item is available. Sometimes, an item is very popular. We run out of it. You'll see that on the screen, too," she explains.

Martin frowns. "Customers must get upset when the company is out of an item. What do you do?"

Angela answers, "We also have other information on the screen. We know when the item will be available again. We tell the customer that date. If the customer still wants the item, we send it out when it's back in stock."

TALK ABOUT IT

1. Describe two things that Martin will read on the computer screen.

2. You have seen how information can be classified on order forms. Discuss how this would make Martin's job easier when he takes orders over the phone.

Businesses often order items from catalogs. Usually, businesses need fast service. So they fax or phone in their orders.

Order forms from business customers are similar to individual customer order forms. But there are some differences. Business customer order forms ask for some special kinds of information.

Read the business customer order form below. Look for kinds of information that individual customer order forms don't ask for. Then, answer the questions that follow.

purchase (PER-chuhs) **order** code a business customer uses to classify its own orders

---

OFFICE SMART

Customer Information
Company: _____
Name of Person Placing Order: _____
Company Address: _____
City/State/Zip: _____
OFFICE SMART Account Number: _____
Purchase Order Number: _____   Date of Order: _____
Business Telephone Number (Very Important): _____
Computer Type
Windows™ ❑   Macintosh ❑   3.5 Disk ❑   CD-ROM ❑
Items Ordered

Quantity	Item Number	Description	Unit Price	Total
		Subtotal		
		Tax		
		Shipping & Handling*		
		TOTAL		

*10% Shipping & Handling billed on all orders. Minimum $6.50.
Payment Method
Bill us ❑   Check enclosed** ❑
Charge to: VIZA ❑   MajorCard ❑   National Express ❑
Card number: _____   Expiration date: _____
Authorized signature:

_____

Customers who pay by check will receive a 5% **discount
  on their next order.
Order Toll Free: 1-800-555-0000 • Customer Service: 615-555-0001

---

authorized (AW-ther-eyezd) given the right and power to do something

discount (DIHS-kownt) lower price

Answer each question based on the business order form on page 59.

1. The order form lists the business telephone number as being "very important" because Office Smart

    a. must have a completely filled out form.

    b. may need to call the customer with questions about the order.

    c. cannot charge a customer without a telephone number.

    d. will call the customer if there is a discount.

2. If a business pays for its order by check, Office Smart will

    a. charge the customer only $6.50 for shipping and handling.

    b. send the business a bill.

    c. give the business a 5% discount on its next order.

    d. send the business a gift.

3. A business orders three boxes of fax paper. Under what heading would the order clerk write the number of boxes?

    a. Quantity

    b. Description

    c. Unit Price

    d. Total

4. An order clerk needs to look up the charge card account number for a business. In which part of the business order form should the clerk look?

    a. Computer Type

    b. Customer Information

    c. Items Ordered

    d. Payment Method

5. A business calls to check on its order. What information could help the order clerk find it?

Check your answers on page 118.

◆ LESSON WRAP-UP

In this lesson, you saw that information may be classified. *Classifying* means "putting similar information together in groups." The groups may have headings. The headings tell what the information has in common. Classifying information by grouping it under a heading makes it easier to read and understand.

In this lesson, you read two kinds of order forms that order clerks use. Both kinds of order forms classified information under headings.

Knowing how to classify information is a useful skill. It will help you find information much more quickly when you read.

1. Think about the material you read at home, at work, and in school. How will it help you to improve your reading if you can classify information when you read?

Finish the sentence below.

Being able to classify information will help my reading because

2. Think about materials you have read on the job. The job may be one you have now. Or it may be a job you had in the past. What is the job? What did you read? Why was it important to be able to classify information in your reading on the job?

Write a paragraph based on the questions above.

Check your answers on page 118.

CLASSIFYING INFORMATION

Working in an Auto Club

▼▼▼▼▼▼▼▼▼▼▼
Words to Know

compass rose

interchange

interstate

legend

vicinity

Many people who drive join auto clubs. These clubs have assistants who help club members. When members have car trouble, they can call their auto club. Auto club assistants will help members find garages that do auto repairs. Auto club assistants also will arrange for the cars to be towed to the garages.

Auto club assistants help members in other ways. For example, auto club assistants help plan trips. They find the best roads to take and places to stay. They also help members stay safe as they travel.

On the job, auto club assistants read travel information. Some of this information is visual. Road maps, for example, give information in drawings and pictures. **Understanding visual information** takes special reading skills.

In this lesson, you will read the kinds of road maps that auto club assistants read. Using road maps, auto club assistants figure mileage (MYEL-uhg), or the number of miles between two places. They also find the best roads to take and places to stay overnight.

Job Focus

Becoming an **auto club assistant** is one way to begin working in the travel business. Auto club assistants work directly with auto club members. This requires good "people skills." It also requires good speaking skills. To plan trips, auto club assistants must also be skilled map readers.

Auto club assistants are part of a larger group of workers in the travel industry. At this time, about 131,000 people are working as ticket clerks and travel assistants of all kinds. About 40,000 of these people are auto club assistants. As long as people travel by car, there should be a need for auto club assistants.

Understanding Visual Information: How It Works

compass (KAHM-puhs)
rose a map symbol that
shows direction

Auto club assistants read road maps. This requires **understanding visual information,** such as pictures. Road maps use special pictures, called *symbols,* to give information. For example, most road maps include a direction symbol, or **compass rose.** The compass rose tells how to find north, south, east, and west on the map. At the top of the compass rose is the letter *N,* for *north.* You can see that if north is at the top, east is to the right. West is to the left, and south is to the bottom.

Below is a road map of Perth Amboy, a city in New Jersey. This map could be used by an auto club assistant. Look at the roads and places on the map. Then, find the compass rose.

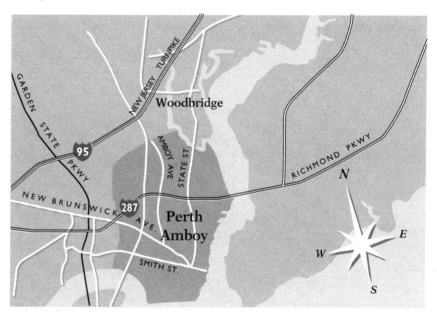

Suppose you want to drive from Perth Amboy to Woodbridge. In what direction is Woodbridge from Perth Amboy?

Woodbridge is *north* of Perth Amboy. Find both cities on the map. Then, look at the compass rose. Since Woodbridge is above Perth Amboy, Woodbridge is to the north.

What road would you take from Perth Amboy to Woodbridge—New Brunswick Ave. or State Street?

The answer is *State Street.* It runs north and south between Perth Amboy and Woodbridge. New Brunswick Ave. does not go north.

Annie wants to drive to the Community College of Rhode Island (CCRI). She goes to her auto club for directions. You are the auto club assistant who talks to Annie.

Annie lives on Mt. Pleasant Ave. in Providence. You know that the college is not far from there. It is in a town called Lincoln. Annie knows that Lincoln is north of Providence. But she needs more information about the best way to get there.

You get a map of Providence and **vicinity** and begin to study it. Look at the map below. Find the compass rose and CCRI. Then, study the **legend**. It is the box that has the symbols (pictures) with descriptions. For example, the route marker ⬡ means U.S. Highway 1. You can use the map, legend, and compass rose to give Annie directions.

Based on the map, answer the questions that follow.

vicinity (vuh-SIHN-uht-ee) a nearby area or neighborhood

legend (LEHJ-uhnd) a list of symbols on a map and their meanings

interstate (IHNT-er-stayt) between two or more states

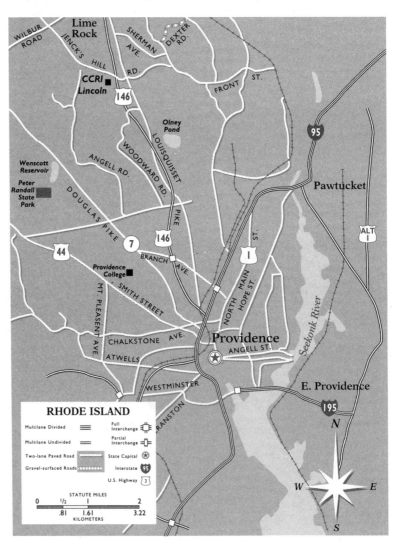

LESSON 8 ◆ WORKING IN AN AUTO CLUB

Answer each question based on the map on page 64.

1. Annie lives on Mt. Pleasant Ave., south of Chalkstone Ave. Driving south on Mt. Pleasant Ave., she will come to

    a. railroad tracks.
    b. an airport.
    c. Providence College.
    d. Atwells Ave.

2. You tell Annie to go east to the Louisquisset Turnpike. Once she reaches the turnpike, she should go

    a. north.
    b. south.
    c. east.
    d. west.

3. Just before Annie gets to the Community College of Rhode Island (CCRI), she will see

    a. Providence College.
    b. Peter Randall State Park.
    c. Olney Pond.
    d. Wenscott Reservoir.

4. From the legend and the map, you know that

    a. Providence is next to the Atlantic Ocean.
    b. Pawtucket is the state capital.
    c. an interstate highway runs through Providence.
    d. Providence is north of Pawtucket.

5. Which of the following streets is closest to the Community College of Rhode Island (CCRI)?

    a. Wilbur Road
    b. Woodward Road
    c. Jenck's Hill Road
    d. Sherman Avenue

6. According to the map and legend, Route 146 is a

    a. multilane, undivided road.
    b. multilane, divided road.
    c. two-lane, paved road.
    d. gravel-surfaced road.

Check your answers on page 119.

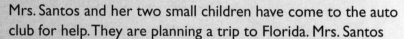

Mrs. Santos and her two small children have come to the auto club for help. They are planning a trip to Florida. Mrs. Santos shows her auto club membership card to the receptionist. The receptionist refers her to the auto club assistant, Brian.

Brian greets the family politely. "Hello," he says. "I am Brian. How may I help you?"

Mrs. Santos says, "We are taking a trip to Florida. Can you help me figure out the best way to drive there?"

Brian asks, "Where are you going in Florida?"

"To Disney World!" shouts the younger girl.

Mrs. Santos says, "As a matter of fact, we are going to visit my mother in Orlando. Isn't Disney World near there?"

Brian answers, "Let's look at a map."

Brian takes out a large map of Florida. "This is where we are now," he explains as he points to Albany, Georgia. "And this is where your mother lives. From the mileage chart, you can see that Orlando is 436 miles from here. From Orlando to Disney World, it is another 20 miles."

Mrs. Santos thinks for a moment. "I may not want to drive all the way to Orlando in one day. Can you help me find some place to stay overnight? I would like a family hotel or motel about half-way to Orlando."

Brian hands Mrs. Santos a booklet that lists hotels and motels. He shows her how to use the booklet to choose a place to stay. Then, he hands her a booklet of safe driving tips. Mrs. Santos now has a map and two booklets to help her plan her trip.

TALK ABOUT IT

1. Describe three kinds of materials that Brian reads on the job.

2. Discuss how Brian uses visual materials to help members. How does he use written materials to help?

interchange (IHN-ter-chaynj) the point at which drivers exit a highway or change from one highway to another

To drive from one state to another, most drivers prefer to travel on interstate highways. To get on an interstate highway, the driver must go through an **interchange.** Drivers can get information about highways and interchanges from a road map.

The road map below includes Albany, Georgia, and Orlando, Florida. It shows the major interstate highways and the key interchanges. An auto club assistant could use this map to help a club member plan a trip from Albany to Orlando.

Look at the map below. Find Albany, Georgia, and Orlando, Florida. Then, use the map to answer the questions that follow.

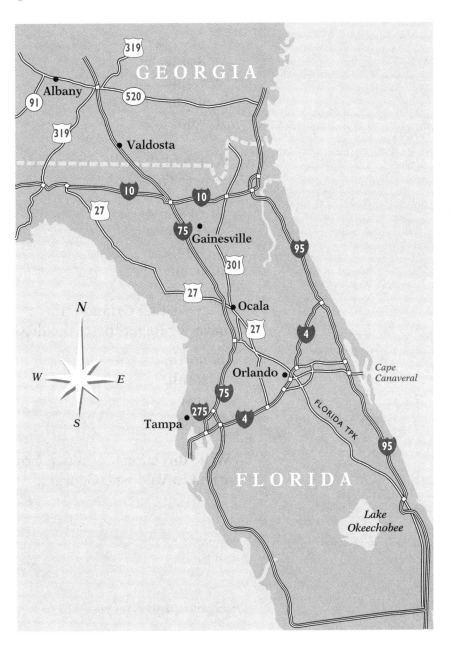

Answer each question based on the map on page 67.

1. A driver wants to stay on the interstate highways as much as possible when driving from Albany to Orlando. Most of the trip, the driver will take

    a. Route 10.
    b. Route 75.
    c. Route 319.
    d. Route 520.

2. What highway route connects Ocala to the Orlando area?

    a. Route 4
    b. Route 275
    c. Route 91
    d. Route 27

3. Which of the following cities is not on the route from Albany to Orlando?

    a. Valdosta
    b. Gainesville
    c. Tampa
    d. Ocala

4. After visiting Orlando, the driver decides to go to Cape Canaveral. To get there, the driver should go

    a. north.
    b. south.
    c. east.
    d. west.

5. Write directions for a trip from Cape Canaveral, Florida, to Valdosta, Georgia.

Check your answers on page 119.

◆ LESSON WRAP-UP

In this lesson, you practiced reading visual information. You looked at road maps that auto club assistants may use. You learned how to read a compass rose and a legend. You saw how these symbols give information in pictures and in words.

The compass rose shows direction. It tells you where north is on a road map. Once you find north, you can use the compass rose to find south, east, and west.

The legend explains the different symbols on the road map. Legends may explain the road system, including the highway interchanges. Legends may explain numbered routes so that drivers can quickly find road signs as they drive. Legends may also point out special areas, such as capital cities and interesting places to visit.

1. Think about maps that you have seen at home, at work, or in school. What other kinds of maps do people read besides road maps?

2. Describe three different times when people might need to read maps.

3. Think of a time when you would need to read a map. It could be at home, at work, or in school. Write a paragraph explaining how it would help you to be able to understand the map.

Check your answers on page 119.

Meeting Customers' Needs

Have you ever opened a checking account at a bank? Have you ever asked for your money back when you didn't like what you bought? Chances are you talked with a customer service representative, or CSR.

The job of the customer service representative is to help customers. For example, a customer may complain that an item he or she bought does not work. To solve the customer's problem, the CSR must be good at **distinguishing fact from opinion.** The item may be broken, or the customer may have used it incorrectly. The CSR must get the facts to make things right.

In this lesson, you will read several kinds of forms that customer service representatives use. You will also practice distinguishing facts from opinions. This important skill will help you when you read.

Job Focus

Customer service representatives help customers who need help or information. They gather information from customers by mail, by telephone, and in person. The information helps businesses meet customers' needs.

CSRs may do a variety of tasks. CSRs may describe products or services to customers. CSRs may also work with customers who have complaints. Whatever the task, the CSR represents the business to its customers.

About 183,000 people work as customer service representatives. More than half of these CSRs work in banks. The job outlook for CSRs is good. Businesses need friendly, helpful people to help meet their customers' needs. There will always be a place for CSRs with good "people skills."

Distinguishing Fact from Opinion: How It Works

Facts are statements that can be proven to be true. *Opinions* are people's beliefs. Opinions vary from person to person. They cannot be proven true or false. Here are some ways to **distinguish fact from opinion.** You can:

- test what is said. If a person says his address is 4 Elm Street, you can check a telephone book for proof.
- watch for clue words that signal an opinion. Example: *"I think* my order was lost in the mail." The word *think* is a clue word that signals an opinion.
- read or listen for statements that are too broad to be fact. Example: *"All* savings accounts are the same."

Customer service representatives need to be good at distinguishing facts from opinions. They use many kinds of forms to gather information from customers. Some questions ask for facts. Others ask for opinions.

The form below is used by a weight loss company. CSRs give this form to new customers. Read the form, and look for facts and opinions.

registration
(rehj-ih-STRAY-shuhn)
enrollment or sign up

⧉⧉⧉⧉⧉ *Registration Form* ⧉⧉⧉⧉⧉

Name _____

Address _____

City/State/Zip Code _____

Other weight loss programs you have been to:

_____

Number of pounds you lost on that program: _____

How do you feel about your weight loss while in the program?

_____

What did you like about the program? What did you dislike?

_____

Which questions would be answered with facts?

_____

The facts called for are *the person's name and address, the names of other weight loss programs, and the number of pounds lost.* These answers can all be proven true.

Which questions ask for opinions?

_____

The last three questions ask for opinions. The words *feel, like* and *dislike* are clue words that tell you that they are opinions.

usinesses want to make sure they are meeting the needs of their customers. Some customers may need more information. Others may have a complaint. They may be unhappy with an item they bought. Customer service representatives work with these customers. They use many kinds of forms to get the information they need.

Below are parts of two different forms customer service representatives read. As you read the forms, try to tell which questions ask for facts and which ask for opinions. Then, answer the questions that follow.

Form 1

> ## Want More Information?
>
> 1. **Yes!** Have a customer service representative call me.
>   Telephone: _____
> 2. Name, Job Title: _____
>   Company: _____
>   Address: _____
>   City/State/Zip: _____
> 3. Computer Type:
>   Windows ❑   Macintosh ❑   3.5 Disk ❑   CD-ROM ❑
> 4. I am (happy/unhappy) with my current computer
>   system because _____
> 5. If I could change my computer system, I would
>   _____

Form 2

merchandise
(MER-chuhn-deyes) goods
that are bought or sold

> ## Merchandise Return Form
>
> Name _____
> Address _____
> City/State/Zip _____
> Your Account Number_____
>
> Reason for Return:
> Was it the size ordered? __   Was it properly packaged? __
> Was it the color ordered?__   Was the item damaged?   __
> Was the quality what you ordered? __   expected?   __
> Comments: _____
> _____

Answer each question based on the forms on page 72.

1. One fact asked for in Form 1 is

   a. the customer's computer type.
   b. the customer service representative's name.
   c. the name of the item the customer wants to buy.
   d. the customer's feelings about the computer system.

2. In Form 1, the customer is asked to give an opinion in

   a. part 1.
   b. part 2.
   c. part 3.
   d. part 5.

3. In Form 1, there is a clue that tells you that part 4 asks for an opinion. It is

   a. the word because.
   b. the blank line for the customer to write on.
   c. the words happy and unhappy.
   d. the word I.

4. From the Reason for Return part in Form 2, which question calls for the customer's opinion?

   a. Was it the size ordered?
   b. Was it properly packaged?
   c. Was it the color ordered?
   d. Was the item damaged?

5. In Form 2, which of the following does not have to be answered with a fact?

   a. Address
   b. Your Account Number
   c. Zip Code
   d. Comments

Check your answers on page 119.

Lin was hired by Barry Department Store during the busy holiday season. She would be doing many different things. She would work wherever she was needed.

The woman who hired Lin told her not to worry about learning so many tasks. The tasks would be carefully explained in the employee manual. Lin could read the manual to answer most of her questions.

As it turned out, this job was great experience for Lin. She worked in almost every department. Lin even worked "behind the scenes" in the office. Lin was surprised that she loved office work. Before working in the office, she thought it would be all typing and filing. Instead, she got the chance to use a computer and help people.

Sometimes, Lin answered phone calls. Some callers just needed information about where the nearest store was. Lin had to read travel directions to these callers. Other times, people called to open charge accounts. Lin had to read computer forms to help them. Some customers called to complain. Lin read customer service information in the employee manual in order to help these customers.

After the holiday season passed, she was offered a job. It seemed that everyone was very happy with Lin's work. They were pleased that she was skilled at customer service. They wanted her to stay to work in the office.

TALK ABOUT IT

1. Describe three kinds of reading that Lin had to do.

2. Tell why you think distinguishing facts from opinions will be an important skill for Lin when she works in the office.

products (PRAHD-uhkts) things that businesses make to sell

services (SUHR-vuhs-ehz) things that businesses do to help customers or other businesses

surveys (SER-vayz) a set of questions asking for facts and opinions

Businesses sell their **products** and **services** to customers. They often ask customers what they think about a product or service. Customer service representatives collect that information. They use the telephone to reach customers. They also mail **surveys** that customers fill out and return. The information is collected and then studied.

Part of a survey is shown below. A car repair shop sends the survey to customers after repair jobs. The repair shop is interested in finding out what opinions their customers have about the repair work. Read the survey and answer the questions that follow.

satisfaction (sat-ihs-FAHK-shuhn) happiness or contentment with a job well done

routine maintenance (roo-TEEN MAYN-tuh-nuhns) regular work to keep something performing well

---

S U R V E Y

Thank you for doing business with Cranwell Repair. Your **satisfaction** is important to us. If there is any way we can serve you better, we want to know about it. Please take a few minutes to fill out this survey. Use the enclosed, stamped envelope to return it to us. Thanks for your time.

1. Your Name _____
2. Address _____
3. City/State/Zip _____
4. Telephone Number: Daytime _____ Evening _____
5. Type of Car _____
6. Repair? _____ or **Routine Maintenance**? _____
7. Date of Repair or Maintenance Appointment _____
8. If you waited for your car, was it taken at the time you had your appointment? _____
9. If you waited for your car, did we make you comfortable?
   _____
10. Was the work finished on time? _____
11. When the car was returned to you, had it been washed? ___
12. Did you find our front desk people helpful when you
    • called for an appointment? _____
    • picked up the car? _____
    • had questions? _____
13. How would you rate our overall service? (Choose one.)
    Poor   Fair   Good   Very Good
14. Would you return for service again?
    _____
    _____

Answer each question based on the survey on page 75.

1. Which of the following questions calls for the customer's opinion?

    a. Was your car taken at the time you had your appointment?

    b. Were you having repair work or routine maintenance work done on your car?

    c. When the car was returned to you, had it been washed?

    d. How would you rate our overall service?

2. In answer to Item 9 on the survey, a customer claims the seats in the waiting room were too dirty to sit on. You know that

    a. it is a fact that the seats could not be used.

    b. the customer was giving an opinion.

    c. the customer was unhappy with the repairs on his car.

    d. all customers agree that the seats were too dirty.

3. Which of the following is a fact because it can be checked?

    a. whether the car can go another 10,000 miles on its original tires

    b. whether the people at the front desk were helpful

    c. the date of the repair or maintenance appointment

    d. whether the customer would return to the company for future car repairs

4. A customer answers "Yes" to Item 10. Which of the following tells you the customer's answer was a fact?

    a. A repair order shows that a customer was told the car would be ready at 3 P.M. The order shows that the customer picked up the car at 2:30 P.M.

    b. A note from the customer service representative shows that a customer called to complain about how long the repair was taking.

    c. A phone message shows that the customer called to tell the company to go ahead with the oil change.

    d. A repair manual says that this kind of repair usually takes two hours.

Check your answers on page 119.

◆ LESSON WRAP-UP

In this lesson, you learned how to distinguish fact from opinion. Facts can be proven to be true. Opinions are beliefs that cannot be proven. To tell the difference between facts and opinions you can:

- test what is said
- watch for words that signal an opinion
- read or listen for statements that are too broad to be fact

Distinguishing fact from opinion is an important reading skill. You used this skill when reading forms such as surveys and merchandise return forms.

Customer service representatives need to distinguish fact from opinion when helping customers. Businesses also need to distinguish fact from opinion when trying to improve service. They often use surveys to find out what customers think about their services and products.

1.Think about the material you read at home, at work, and in school. How will it help you to improve your reading if you can distinguish fact from opinion?

Finish the sentence below.

Being able to distinguish fact from opinion will help my reading because

2. Think about the reading you have done on the job. The job may be one you have now, or it may be a job you had in the past. What is the job? What did you read? Why was it important to be able to distinguish fact from opinion?

Write a paragraph based on the questions above.

Check your answers on page 119.

◆ UNIT THREE REVIEW

1. How can classifying information help you understand what you are reading?

2. Write a strategy for reading and understanding a map.

3. How is a fact different from an opinion?

4. Think of the jobs that you learned about in this unit. Which job interests you the most? Why are you interested in this job? How could you learn more about it? Why would it be important to have good reading skills for this job?

Write a paragraph based on these questions.

Check your answers on page 119.

Unit Four

· Jobs in Finance ·

In business, there are many workers whose jobs have to do with money. Some actually handle money. Others make sure that money is collected from customers on time.

In this unit, you will read about three kinds of finance (FEYE-nans) workers. Bank tellers actually handle money. They help customers deposit and withdraw money. Credit clerks help customers set up charge accounts with businesses. Billing clerks use many records to prepare bills for customers.

All these workers read many kinds of forms and records. They also read letters, memos, and policies. There are many rules for handling finances. These workers must be able to read to find the information they need to do their jobs.

This unit teaches the following reading skills:

- ◆ identifying cause and effect
- ◆ drawing conclusions
- ◆ finding details that support the main idea

You will learn how finance workers use these reading skills in their work.

Working as a Bank Teller

▼▼▼▼▼▼▼▼▼▼▼▼

Words to Know

balance

convenience

financial

interest

lines of credit

transactions

Think of your last visit to a bank. Did you take money out of your account? If so, you probably filled out a withdrawal (wihth-DRAW-uhl) slip. If you added money to your account, you probably filled out a deposit (dih-PAHZ-uht) slip. You then gave the slip, or form, to a bank teller.

Bank tellers help customers. They also handle paperwork. They check deposit and withdrawal slips to see that they are correct. They carefully add or subtract the right amount from customers' accounts. Bank tellers also keep records of deposits and withdrawals.

To do their jobs, bank tellers must be good at **identifying cause and effect.** Each time a customer makes a deposit or withdrawal, the amount of money in their account is affected.

In this lesson, you will read materials that bank tellers read. As you read, you will practice identifying cause and effect.

Job Focus

Because **bank tellers** work with money, they need good math skills. They must carefully count money to avoid errors. They also need good computer skills. Banks use computers to keep records of deposits and withdrawals. Tellers use computers to give bank customers information about their accounts.

Good "people skills" also are important. Bank tellers listen to customers. They talk to customers to answer questions and explain banking services. They must know a lot about the banking services their bank offers.

About 559,000 people work as bank tellers. Over one fourth of these tellers work part time.

Identifying Cause and Effect: How It Works

A **cause** is an action that leads to a result. The result is the **effect.** For example, a customer writes a check to a store for more money than he has in his bank account. What will happen? The check will bounce. In other words, the bank cannot pay the store the amount on the check. In this case, the cause is writing a check for more than is in the account. The effect is that the bank will not pay the check.

When you read, you must understand how causes lead to effects. Remember that a cause is an action that leads to a result, or effect.

Read the memo below. Look for cause and effect as you read.

M E M O

Date: November 27
To: All Bank Staff
From: Meg Reilly, Head Teller
Subject: Problems with Personal Identification Numbers

We have recently had problems with customers and their use of personal identification numbers (PINs). The PINs makes it more difficult for someone to misuse a stolen or lost bank card.

We must encourage customers to use their PINs properly. Please warn customers to keep their PINs a secret. Tell them never to tell their PINs to anyone, including a bank employee. They should not write their PINs on their bank cards. Also, warn them against using their birthdays, phone numbers, or address numbers as their PINs. These are the first numbers someone will try with a stolen or lost card. If customers keep their PINs a secret, their money will be safe.

The memo tells three causes that could lead to customers' losing money from their accounts. What are these causes?

_____

_____

The three causes are *(1) telling their PIN to others, (2) writing their PIN on the bank cards,* and *(3) using birthdays, phone numbers, or address numbers as their PIN.*

Each of these causes could lead to the same effect— having money stolen from an account.

Bank tellers handle many different kinds of tasks. They accept deposits and withdrawals. Tellers also are a part of the bank's sales team. They help sell bank products and services to bank customers.

Pamphlets (PAM-fluhts) are short booklets that banks give to customers. They help customers understand how to use the bank's services. Tellers also read these materials.

Below is part of a pamphlet about bank cards. Read the pamphlet. Then, answer the questions that follow.

convenience
(kuhn-VEEN-yuhns) ease of use; something that makes a task less difficult

transactions
(tranz-AK-shuhnz) business exchanges; for example, providing a product in exchange for money

balance (BAL-uhns) amount of money that is left in a bank account

Banking **Convenience** For You

Your Superbank Bank Card will help you in many ways. It will make banking easier. Superbank isn't open 24 hours a day. But our automated teller machines (ATMs) are. You can always get the cash you need at any hour of any day.

Most people need to do many different **transactions.** The Bank Card will help you to do them. For example, suppose you need to make a deposit or find out your **balance**. Your Bank Card is all you need.

At your request, we recently added three new transactions. You can now use your Bank Card to:

- Transfer Money
- Make a Loan Payment
- Cash a Check

There are many places you can use your Bank Card. You will find Superbank ATMs at easy-to-reach places all over the state. We are now in your local supermarkets, too. And, for a small fee, you can also use ATMs at other banks, such as Ace and Big Bank. If you are traveling outside the United States, we have the Superbank System that lets you cash a check. There is no charge to Superbank customers for any of these services at any of our 15,000 locations.

Answer each question based on the pamphlet on page 82.

1. One effect of having a Bank Card is that a customer can

    a. get cash only at Superbank ATMs.

    b. only get cash in the United States.

    c. do many different transactions at any time of day.

    d. decide to travel even more.

2. Customers will be charged a fee to use their Superbank Bank Card when they

    a. use the Bank Card at a supermarket.

    b. cash a check outside the United States.

    c. make a loan payment.

    d. use ATMs at other banks.

3. The effect of having automated teller machines open 24 hours a day is that customers will

    a. use other ATMs from other banks more often.

    b. be able to get cash at any time.

    c. perform more transactions at night instead of during the day.

    d. cash checks more often.

4. The effect of having Superbank ATMs outside the United States is that customers will know that they

    a. can always get money from their accounts when they travel.

    b. should always carry enough cash with them on a trip.

    c. can deposit money in a Superbank account at any hour of the day.

    d. can afford to travel more often.

5. Why did Superbank add three new transactions to its Bank Card service?

    a. Bank cards from other companies had more services than Superbank had.

    b. Customers who traveled outside the United States complained.

    c. Customers asked the bank to add more transactions.

    d. Adding more transactions saved the bank money.

Check your answers on page 120.

When Patrick took the job at Northeast Bank, he thought all he would do is cash checks and make deposits. But he soon learned that there was much more to being a bank teller.

Most of the new things Patrick learned were covered in his job manual. In it, he learned the correct steps for every type of transaction. Everything had more steps than he expected. To cash a check, he followed five steps:

- Verify, or make sure, that the date is correct.
- Check the bank name.
- Check the identity of the person cashing the check.
- Check the amounts written on the check—both in words and numbers.
- Check whether the bank account has enough money in it to cover the check.

Besides learning about transactions, Patrick learned all about the services the bank offered. He studied the pamphlets that the bank gave its customers. He would need to be prepared to answer their questions.

In his job manual, Patrick also learned important steps for handling cash. Each morning, he would receive his cash drawer. His first job was to count the cash. His supervisor would make sure that the count was correct. Then, after the bank closed, he would count the cash left in his drawer. Patrick had to show that the money in his drawer matched the written records of the transactions he did that day.

Patrick was glad to see that his new job would keep him very busy. He looked forward to learning more about banking.

TALK ABOUT IT

1. Describe the kinds of reading Patrick did to learn his job.

2. Explain why reading is an important skill for a bank teller.

Bank tellers often take courses to learn new skills. In some courses, manuals give the tellers material to read and study. Tellers can use the manuals to reread instructions that they're not sure about.

Look at a section from a training manual below. The section introduces the bank's new service to the owners of small businesses. Read the manual. Then, answer the questions that follow.

SMALL BUSINESSES' SPECIAL NEEDS

○ Customers who own small businesses have special banking needs. At Central Bank, we offer the services that meet those needs. What is really different about our services is you. After you complete this training, you will be able to explain our services to our business customers.

Here are some of the services that you will be talking to customers about:

■ Special checking accounts that are planned especially for small business owners. Thanks to our new account planning software, we can set up the best kind of account for each customer.

■ New check printing service. This service will help to keep costs down for our customers. Whether a customer writes many checks or only a few, the customer will save money with us.

○ ■ **Lines of credit** at a low rate of **interest**.

■ Short-term loans for buying equipment. These are usually 1- to 5-year loans.

Many of our customers ask what they will need to bring when they apply for credit. To help them plan ahead, we have prepared The Credit Planning Worksheet. It tells the small business owner what information is needed to apply for credit. Here is the information needed:

■ The number of years in business
■ The kind of business it is
■ The number of people employed by the business
■ How much money the owner would like to borrow
■ The owner's plans for helping the business to grow
○ ■ The reason for the loan
■ A **financial** statement and tax return for the business

---

lines of credit (KREHD-iht) money available to borrow, up to a certain limit

interest (IHN-trihst) charges on a loan for the use of the bank's money; also, money that a bank pays savers for the use of their money

financial (fuh-NAN-chuhl) having to do with money

Answer each question based on the training manual on page 85.

1. The bank hopes that after the training, tellers will

   a. tell business customers to talk to a manager.
   b. make fewer errors when they count money.
   c. have better computer skills.
   d. explain banking services to business customers.

2. The bank claims it can now set up the best kind of account for each customer. What is the cause of this improvement?

   a. the new training program for managers
   b. the new account planning software
   c. hiring tellers with better computer skills
   d. the new check printing service

3. Because many customers asked what they needed to bring to apply for credit, the bank

   a. prepared the Credit Planning Worksheet.
   b. bought new computer software.
   c. started this training program for bank tellers.
   d. set up many special accounts for business customers.

4. Which piece of information is not needed by a small business owner to apply for credit?

   a. the reason the owner needs the loan
   b. how many people work at the business
   c. the checking account records for the business
   d. the amount of money the owner wants to borrow

5. The bank says it can save the customer money on checks. What is the cause?

   a. The bank does not charge its customers for checking account services.
   b. The bank has its own check printing service.
   c. The bank has new computer software for handling accounts.
   d. The bank has a low rate of interest for a line of credit.

Check your answers on page 120.

◆ LESSON WRAP-UP

In this lesson, you learned how to identify cause and effect in what you read. You learned that a cause is an action that leads to an effect. The cause is the reason that the effect happens.

You identify cause and effect all the time. For example, you may have asked yourself, "What will happen if I don't go to school today?" When you ask yourself a question like this, you are figuring out the effect of your actions. This skill is useful no matter what job you have.

Bank tellers also need to be able to identify cause and effect. For example, they need to understand how their services affect the success of their bank.

1. Think about the material that you read at home, at work, and in school. How will it help you to improve your reading if you can identify cause and effect when you read?

Finish the sentence below.

Identifying the cause and effect in reading material will help my reading because

2. Think about the reading materials that you have read on a job. The job may be one that you have now. Or it may be a job that you had in the past. What is the job? What did you read? Why was it important to identify cause and effect in what you read on the job?

Write a paragraph based on the questions above.

Check your answers on page 120.

Checking Credit Information

Sometimes people want to buy something that costs more than they can afford all at once. For example, a person may be shopping for a new TV. If the TV costs a lot, the person might decide to "buy it on time" and apply for credit. That way, the person could make smaller payments instead of one large payment.

To apply for credit, the person might talk to a credit clerk. The clerk would have the person fill out a special form called a credit application. The credit clerk also would answer questions that the person might ask.

If the person asked a lot of questions, the credit clerk might conclude that the person never before applied for credit. Based on this conclusion, the clerk would offer extra help. **Drawing conclusions** is part of a credit clerk's job.

In this lesson, you will read a memo about the work that credit clerks do. You also will read different kinds of credit applications. As you read, you will practice drawing conclusions.

Job Focus

Credit clerks must be good with details. They carefully check the details on credit applications. They also need good "people skills." Credit clerks call applicants, employers, banks, and others to check that information on applications is true.

Credit clerks work in department stores, insurance offices, and in real estate offices. These clerks may work directly with applicants. Credit clerks also work for credit bureaus. These businesses check information on credit applications for banks and other businesses.

About 258,000 people work in the credit field. This number includes both credit clerks and other workers.

Drawing Conclusions: How It Works

When you **draw a conclusion** you make a judgment or decision based on facts you read. Conclusions also are based on your own knowledge and experiences.

Drawing conclusions involves three steps. First, you gather new facts. These are the facts you read. Next, you recall "old facts"—what you already know. Finally, you think about the facts to make a judgment or decision.

Credit clerks need to draw conclusions when they work with credit applications. When they do, they follow the same three steps. Read the following memo that credit clerks in a department store received.

verify (VEHR-uh-feye) check information to make sure that it is true

authorizers (AW-thuhr-eyez-uhrz) credit workers who approve giving credit to people

> TO: All Credit Clerks
> FROM: Rudy Padjima, Credit Manager
> DATE: December 1
> SUBJECT: Credit Applications
> This is our busiest time of year. I know that you have extra work to do. But please—do not take shortcuts! You must **verify** the information on <u>every</u> application. **Authorizers** make credit decisions based on this information. The authorizers are counting on us.
>
> People can be hard to reach at this time of year. If you cannot reach an employer to verify how much an applicant earns, do not skip that detail. Instead, tell me. Together, we'll decide what to do.

Why might the credit clerks be extra busy? Draw a conclusion based on the date of the memo. Recall what you already know about this time of year.

_____

If you said that the credit clerks are extra busy *because it is the holiday season,* you are right. It is December, and many people buy gifts during this month. As a result, more people apply for credit.

What mistake might the authorizers make if the credit clerks do not verify information?

_____

_____

references (REHF-uhr-uhns-ehz) people or businesses in a position to recommend another; statements about a person's dependability

dependents (dih-PEHN-duhnts) people who depend, or rely on, others to pay for their living expenses, such as children or adults who do not work

co-applicant (KOH-ap-lih-kuhnt) person who will share the account

authorized (AW-thuh-reyezd) allowed or given the power to do something

You are right if you said that *the authorizers might give credit to people who cannot afford it.* Authorizers use information on applications to make credit decisions. If this information is false, the authorizers will make bad decisions.

The form below is part of a credit application for a store credit card. A credit clerk will read the form and check the information. The clerk will check whether the form is complete and the information makes sense. Based on this information, the clerk will draw a conclusion about whether to call the applicant for more information.

Read the form. Then, answer the questions that follow.

WARREN'S DEPARTMENT STORE CREDIT APPLICATION

Check one: I want an individual account ☐   A joint account ☒
(Note: You may apply for either whether you are single, married, or separated.)

ABOUT YOU

Name (first, middle, last): Janice B. Utley
Social security number: 051-99-5478
Date of Birth: 3/4/67
Address: 211 N. Park St.   Midway   LA   71006
          Street   City   State   ZIP
Length of time at address: 2 years
Own: ☐   Rent: ☒   Relative's: ☐   Other: ☐
Home phone: (318) 555-5161
Number of **dependents**: 1
Employer: Whitney Bank
Position: Teller   Length of time: 4 years
Work phone: _____
Driver's license number/State: L7340340/LA

ABOUT YOUR BANKING AND CREDIT REFERENCES

Bank name/branch: Whitney Bank
Checking account number: 20034-90653
Bank name/branch: _____
Savings account number: _____
VIZA account number: 314-567-800-455
MajorCard account number: _____
Other: _____
Store or company names: Suters
Account Numbers: 311-67390

ABOUT YOUR (check one)

Co-applicant: ☐
Name: _____
Address: _____
         Street   City   State   ZIP
Relation to applicant: _____
Home phone: _____
Employer: _____
Signature(s) *Janice B. Utley*
              Applicant

Authorized user: ☐
Social security number: _____
Driver's license number/State: _____

Work phone: _____
Length of time: _____
7/8
Date

Other signature (where needed) _____   Date _____

Answer each question based on the application on page 90.

1. What can you conclude from the fact that the joint account box was checked?

    a. The applicant is married or was married at some time.

    b. The form is either incomplete or filled out incorrectly.

    c. The applicant does not make enough money to get a credit card by herself.

    d. The applicant has other joint accounts.

2. You can conclude that the applicant has had credit before because the applicant

    a. checked the joint account box.

    b. works at a bank.

    c. gave a VIZA account number.

    d. signed and dated the form.

3. What can you conclude about the applicant's banking references?

    a. She has never had a savings account.

    b. Her savings account is in her husband's name.

    c. She has two savings accounts.

    d. Her bank account is at the same place that she works.

4. Which of the following facts can you know from the information on the form?

    a. The applicant lived at her current address for four years.

    b. The applicant has a Suters charge account.

    c. The applicant got her VIZA account from Whitney Bank.

    d. The applicant worked in a department store for four years.

5. Does the credit clerk need to call the applicant for more information? Why or why not?

Check your answers on page 120.

It is Hilda's first day as a credit clerk at C&J Credit Bureau. Hilda has two years' experience as a credit clerk in a department store. She knows the basics of the credit clerk's job. But Hilda still has a lot to learn. In her old job, she worked with store customers. In her new job, she will work with banks. Hilda's boss, Catherine, met with Hilda to talk.

Catherine said, "Hilda, you'll find some things about this job are the same as your old job. You used to verify information on store credit applications, right?" Hilda nodded. "Well," Catherine continued, "you'll still do verifying. But instead of working directly with the applicants, you'll work with banks. People apply for different kinds of loans—mortgage loans for buying homes, auto loans, education loans, and so on. Banks hire us to verify information about loan applicants."

Hilda said, "So I'll still be calling employers, landlords, and others to check out information."

"You surely will," said Catherine. "But you'll talk with the bank people rather than the applicants themselves. You'll learn more about the job in this afternoon's training class." Catherine handed Hilda a training manual. "You'll be using this manual in the class. Please read the first two chapters now. That will prepare you."

TALK ABOUT IT

1. Think about the kinds of reading Hilda will do on the job. Describe two of them.

2. Explain why drawing conclusions while reading is important for Hilda.

All applications are not the same. They often ask for some information that may not apply to every applicant. In these cases, the applicant will write "NA." This stands for "not applicable" and means that this item does not apply to the applicant.

Below is part of an auto loan application. Tilmon Bank has hired the C&J Credit Bureau to verify the loan information. Read the application. Then, answer the questions that follow.

term (tuhrm) amount of time given to repay a loan

APPLICATION FOR AUTO LOAN

Amount requested: $7,000   **Term**: 24 months

Do you have a savings account here? Yes ☒   No ☐

Subtract monthly payment from account? Yes ☐   No ☒

Year of vehicle: 94   Make/Model: Venus Roadrider

Sale price: $8,000   Down payment: $1,000

Secured by vehicle? (Applies only to new vehicles) Yes ☐   No ☒

Secured by certificate of deposit (CD)?   Yes ☒   No ☐

Amount of CD: $10,000   CD number: _____

Credit Insurance

I am interested in buying:

Life insurance ☐   Accident & health insurance ☐

Note: You do not need to buy credit insurance to get a loan.

Applicant Information

Name: _America L. Ramos_____
          First/Middle Initial/Last

Date of birth: 10/22/78

Social security number: 123-55-0000

Present address: 8 S. Fairfax Ave. San Diego, CA 92104
          Street   City   State ZIP

Telephone number: _____

Own ☐   Rent ☐   Living with parents ☒

Monthly rental payments: NA

Landlord: (Name and Phone) NA

Current employer: Asia Imports

Job title: Shipping Clerk

Employer phone: (619) 555-3778

Gross yearly income: $21,500

Signature: *America L. Ramos*   Date: 6/5

landlord (LAND-lawrd) a person who owns and rents out apartments or homes to others

Answer each question based on the application on page 93.

1. From the information on the application, you can conclude that "secure a loan" means to
   a. back up the amount of a loan with something of equal or greater value.
   b. request that loan payments be subtracted from a checking account.
   c. be certain that an applicant will receive a loan.
   d. promise to repay a loan over the agreed-upon term.

2. After checking the application to make sure it is filled out correctly, a clerk can conclude that the applicant
   a. has forgotten to fill out the credit insurance section.
   b. has filled out the application completely.
   c. needs to fill in her CD number.
   d. does not have a job.

3. Which of the following facts is *not* required on the application?
   a. the applicant's gross yearly income
   b. the amount the applicant wants to borrow
   c. the applicant's date of birth
   d. the amount of education the applicant has completed

4. From the facts in the Applicant Information section, you can conclude that the applicant
   a. does not have any plans to get her own apartment or house.
   b. used to own her own house.
   c. does not have an employer who can be called to check the amount of gross income.
   d. does not pay rent.

5. You can conclude that the applicant does not
   a. have any children.
   b. want to pay for credit insurance.
   c. have a savings account.
   d. need to secure the loan.

Check your answers on page 120.

◆ LESSON WRAP-UP

In this lesson, you learned how to draw conclusions when you read. To draw conclusions, you practiced three steps. First, you gathered new facts from what you read. Next, you recalled "old facts"—what you already know. Last, you thought about the facts to make a judgment.

People fill out applications to apply for credit. Credit clerks check the applications to make sure that they are complete. They also check the information on credit applications. Credit clerks draw conclusions about whether they need to get more information from applicants. They also draw conclusions about the meaning of information on applications.

1. Think about the material that you read at home, at work, and in school. How will it help you to improve your reading if you can draw conclusions from what you read?

Finish the sentence below.

Being able to draw conclusions from what I read will help me by

2. Think about materials that you have read on a job. The job may be one that you have now, or it may be a job that you had in the past. What is the job? What did you read? Why was it important for you to draw conclusions in the materials you read on the job?

Write a paragraph based on the questions above.

Check your answers on page 120.

L e s s o n   12

Preparing Bills

▼▼▼▼▼▼▼▼▼▼▼

Words to Know

credit

finance charges

grace period

invoice

minimum

posted

remittance

statement of account

terms

Billing clerks work in all kinds of businesses. They prepare the bills that are sent out to customers. Bills are sent to customers to remind them that they owe money to businesses. The money owed may be for products, like clothing, or services, like medical care.

Billing clerks keep records, figure out charges, and correct errors. They read memos, bills, and other paperwork. Billing clerks also read billing policies. These policies explain the rules that a business follows in billing its customers. When a business's billing rules change, the billing clerk makes changes on the customers' bills.

To do their jobs well, billing clerks need detailed information. Main ideas give them general instructions. But main ideas alone are not enough. Billing clerks need to know "specifics," such as who bought what and how much it cost. These are the details that support the main idea. **Finding supporting details** helps billing clerks better understand main ideas.

Job Focus

Billing clerks prepare bills for customers. They look at purchases and figure out the total amount due from a customer. Billing clerks also keep files that show payments.

In a small business, billing clerks may gather billing information from paper records. In larger businesses, billing information is stored on computers. Using the computer system, billing clerks gather billing information and prepare bills. Computer skills can be very important in this job.

About 323,000 people work as billing clerks. Many are employed by banks, insurance companies, and stores. There will be many job openings through the year 2005.

Finding Supporting Details: How It Works

Most things that you read have a main idea. Supporting details are specific facts and ideas that support, or explain, the main idea. They often answer the questions *who? what? when? where? why?* and *how?* **Finding supporting details** in a reading will help you better understand the main idea.

Below is a bill that was prepared by a billing clerk. This type of bill has many details. It is sent each month to customers who have used their credit cards to buy items. Read the statement of account.

statement (STAYT-muhnt) **of account** (uh-KOWNT) a detailed bill that describes transactions that occurred over a period of time

finance (FEYE-nans) **charges** fees that are charged when customers do not pay their bills in full by the due date

minimum (MIHN-uh-muhm) the smallest amount allowed

Phillips Department Store

August **Statement of Account**

Please pay the new balance by the payment due date to avoid **finance charges.**

Billing Date   08/20   Payment Due Date 09/14
To: May Cummings   Customer Charge Account # 6J7039
Address: 278 First Street
Fayette, IL 62044

Date of Purchase	Description	Charge
07/30	Housewares	69.95
08/17	Shoes	42.80

Previous Balance	$0.00	Finance Charge	$0.00
New Balance	$112.75	**Minimum** Payment	$11.27

The first sentence states the main idea: *Please pay the new balance by the payment due date to avoid any finance charges.* Simply put, this means, "Please pay your bill on time."

Which supporting detail tells the customer exactly *when* she must pay her bill?

_____

The customer's bill should be paid by the *Payment Due Date,* which is *09/14.*

How much does the customer need to pay?

_____

The customer needs to pay at least the *Minimum Payment* of *$11.27* by the due date.

Each of these supporting details gives the customer more information.

A statement of account is a record of a customer's purchases and payments. It also shows how much the customer owes. To prepare a statement, the billing clerk gets information from computer or paper records. Read the memo and statement below.

M E M O

Date: March 19
To: Angel Brewer, Billing Clerk
From: Gail Johnson, Customer Service
Subject: Monthly Statement for John Bowen

We made a mistake on the February statement for John Bowen. I spoke to Mr. Bowen on the phone. He said that a payment that he sent did not show up on his statement last month. When I checked Mr. Bowen's file, I saw two mistakes. I found a payment and a purchase that were not **posted** to his account. Please make sure that the following details are on his next statement.

Date	Transaction	Charge	**Credit**
1/14	Payment Received		$150.00
1/15	Purchase, Office Supplies	$35.55	

Mr. Bowen should not receive a finance charge on his account this month. He was not late in paying; we made a mistake.

---

posted (POHST-ehd) recorded a payment or a charge

credit (KREHD-iht) amount that is subtracted from the amount that a customer owes

remittance (rih-MIHT-uhnts) payment sent to a business that supplied a product or service

invoice (IHN-vois) detailed list of products and services that were purchased and their costs

---

White and Morgan Office Supplies Statement

To: John Bowen 1035 Sweetzer Ave. Waltham, MA 02154
Account Number: 75-104-JB   Date: March 20
Enclosed is a payment for $ _____
Please detach and return with your **remittance**.

- -

Payment due date: April 14

Invoice Date	**Invoice Number**	Transaction	Charge	Credit
01/14		Payment Received		$150.00
01/15	465	Office Supplies	35.55	
03/07		Payment Received		50.00

Previous Balance	Payments	Purchases	Finance Charge	New Balance Total
$205.89	$200.00	$35.55	$0.00	$41.44

To avoid finance charges, please pay your new balance total by the payment due date.

Answer each question based on the memo and statement on page 98.

1. The main idea of the memo is that the company made a mistake on John Bowen's February statement. What was the mistake?

a. A payment and a purchase were left off the statement.

b. The customer was charged the wrong amount for a purchase.

c. The date of the statement was wrong.

d. The payment due date was left off the statement.

2. The mistake was the company's and not the customer's. So Ms. Johnson asked the billing clerk to make sure that Mr. Bowen

a. received a statement in March.

b. was not charged for office supplies he bought in January.

c. was given extra time to make his March payment.

d. did not receive a finance charge on his March statement.

3. If Mr. Bowen wants to pay the complete bill, what amount should he send to White and Morgan Office Supplies?

a. $205.89   c. $41.44
b. $200.00   d. $35.55

4. Mr. Bowen can find out more about the purchase he made on January 15 by checking Invoice Number

a. 1035.   c. 279.
b. 465.   d. 150.

5. Which of the following dates tells when Mr. Bowen's most recent payment was received by the company?

a. March 20   c. 01/14
b. 03/07   d. April 14

6. How might the details on a statement of account be helpful to a customer?

Check your answers on page 121.

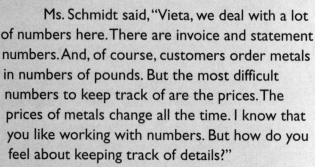

Vieta applied for a billing clerk's job because she likes working with numbers. She interviewed at a company that sells metals. Ms. Schmidt, the head of the Human Resources Department, talked to her. Ms. Schmidt wanted to find out more about Vieta.

Ms. Schmidt said, "Vieta, we deal with a lot of numbers here. There are invoice and statement numbers. And, of course, customers order metals in numbers of pounds. But the most difficult numbers to keep track of are the prices. The prices of metals change all the time. I know that you like working with numbers. But how do you feel about keeping track of details?"

"Well," answered Vieta, "I like keeping details in order. Will I have to figure out total costs, too?"

Ms. Schmidt said, "Yes, you will need to do some math on the job. We have charts that show prices. How do you feel about math?"

Vieta answered, "Math was my best subject. I just need to learn how to fill out the billing forms correctly."

Ms. Schmidt said, "We have sample billing forms and a job manual that explains how to use each form. Of course, you could also ask your supervisor for help. Soon, we will be getting a new computer program. It will store all our customers' names, figure out the total cost, and print out the billing forms."

Ms. Schmidt continued, "But let's see how you do without the computer. I have a sample of our billing form here. Try filling it out. I will give you a price list and some details about the customer. Let's see what you can do with this."

TALK ABOUT IT

1. What kinds of materials will Vieta read if she gets the job?

2. Explain why finding supporting details is important on this job.

terms (tuhrmz) the rules or conditions that a customer and a company have agreed upon

A billing clerk has to understand the company's billing rules, or policies. Different companies have different policies. From time to time, the billing policies may change. Often, there are changes in the **terms**. These are used to figure out the finance charges that a customer owes. The number of days that a customer has to pay the bill may also change.

The following memo explains some changes in a business's billing policies. The billing clerks will be expected to understand and use the new policies. Read the memo. Then, answer the questions that follow.

THE ANIMAL DOCTOR

Date: May 25
To: Billing Department Staff
From: Dr. Anderson
Subject: Changes in Billing Policies

Animal care can be costly. Many of our pet owners want the best for their pets. But they cannot afford to pay the bill all at once. To better meet their needs, we changed our billing policy last year. We began letting customers make smaller payments on the total amount owed.

To meet our own costs, we need to encourage customers to pay their bills as soon as they can. For this reason, we will be changing our policies.

Starting June 1, we will follow these rules:
- Customers will have a 30-day **grace period** to pay their bills. If the bill is paid on time, they will not have to pay any finance charge.
- If the bill is not paid in full in 30 days, we will charge a 1% finance charge on the unpaid amount.
- After 60 days, we will charge a 2% finance charge on the unpaid amount.
- After 90 days, we will charge a 5% finance charge on the unpaid amount. We also will need these customers to pay in full for any future service at the time of the office visit.

We will be sending our customers a letter that explains the new billing policy. Please be prepared to answer their questions. If you do not understand the new policy, please call me. I'll go over it with you.

---

grace (grays) **period** a period of time during which customers do not receive finance charges for money owed

Answer each question based on the memo on page 101.

1. Why is Dr. Anderson changing the billing policy?
    a. to cut back on the number of customers
    b. to better meet the needs of customers
    c. to encourage customers to pay their bills as soon as possible
    d. to help customers take better care of their pets

2. According to the supporting details, the business will not require a finance charge of customers who
    a. pay their bills within 30 days.
    b. pay their bills within 60 days.
    c. pay their bills within 90 days.
    d. make a small payment on their account.

3. Once a bill has gone unpaid for 90 days, the office will
    a. give the customer a 30-day grace period to pay the bill.
    b. charge the customer a 1% finance charge.
    c. give service only if the customer pays any future bill in full at the time of the office visit.
    d. not give service to the customer until the account is paid in full.

4. According to the supporting details, when will these changes take place?
    a. in 60 days
    b. on June 1
    c. on May 25
    d. at the beginning of the year

5. A customer comes into The Animal Doctor to make a payment on her bill of $250. It has been 80 days since she received her bill. What finance charges are being made to her account? What will happen if she doesn't pay the bill within the next 10 days?

Check your answers on page 121.

LESSON WRAP-UP

In this lesson, you learned about supporting details. These specific facts and ideas tell more about the main idea. As you learned, supporting details answer the questions who? what? when? where? why? and how? By finding supporting details, you better understand the main idea.

You also learned that billing clerks prepare bills for customers. To do so, they read and follow their businesses' billing policies. They also read memos and statements of account. Finding supporting details is an important skill for billing clerks. The main idea alone does not give them enough information to do their job well.

1. Think about the material that you read at home, at work, and in school. How will finding supporting details help you improve your reading?

Finish the sentence below.
Finding supporting details will improve my reading by

2. Think about the materials that you have read on a job. The job may be one that you have now, or it may be a job that you had in the past. What is the job? What did you read? Why was it important to find the supporting details in what you read on the job?

Write a paragraph based on the questions above.

Check your answers on page 121.

◆ UNIT FOUR REVIEW

1. Explain the relationship between a cause and an effect.

2. Write about a time when you used facts that you knew to draw a conclusion.

3. Why are supporting details important in a reading?

4. Think of the jobs that you learned about in this unit. Which job interests you the most? Why are you interested in this job? How could you learn more about it? Why would it be important to have good reading skills for this job?

Write a paragraph based on these questions.

Check your answers on page 121.

RESPELLING GUIDE

Use the following guide to help you pronounce long and hard words.

Sound	Respelling	Example of Respelling
a as in hat	a	hat
a as in day, date, paid	ay	day, dayt, payd
vowels as in far, on, bother, hot	ah	fahr, ahn, BAH-thuhr, haht
vowels as in dare, air, heir	ai	dair, air, air
vowels as in saw, call, pore, door	aw	saw, kawl, pawr, dawr
e as in pet, debt	eh	peht, deht
e as in seat, beef, chief, **y** as in beauty	ee	seet, beef, cheef BYOO-tee
vowels as in learn, urn, fur, sir	er	lern, ern, fer, ser
i as in sit, bitter, **ee** as in been	ih	siht, BIHT-uhr, bihn
i as in mile, **ei** as in height	eye	meyel, heyet
o as in go	oh	goh
vowels as in boil, toy	oi	boil, toi
vowels as in how, out, bough	ow	how, owt, bow
vowels as in up, come	u	up, kum
vowels as in use, use, bureau, few	yoo	yooz yoose, BYOO-roh, fyoo
vowels as in look, put, foot	oo	look, poot, foot
vowels as in bitt**er**, act**io**n	uh	BIHT-uhr, AK-shuhn

Consonants are respelled as they sound. Here are a few examples.

c as in cat	k	kat
c as in dance	s	dans
ch as in Christmas	k	KRIHS-muhs
g as in gem	j	jehm
s as in laser	z	LAY-zuhr
ph as in phone	f	fohn

RESOURCES

The following organizations and publications may provide more information about the jobs covered in this book.

United States Government
U.S. Department of Labor, Employment, and Training Administration

Adult Training Programs include the following:
Job Training Partnership Act (JTPA)
This program provides job training for disadvantaged adults who face significant employment barriers. For more information, write:

> Office of Employment and Training
> Programs, Room N4469
> U.S. Department of Labor
> 200 Constitution Ave, N.W.
> Washington, DC 20210

ON THE INTERNET: http://www.doleta.gov/programs/programs.htm

Apprenticeship Training
The Bureau of Apprenticeship and Training registers apprenticeship programs in 23 states. It also assists State Apprenticeship Councils in 27 states, the District of Columbia, Puerto Rico, and the U.S. Virgin Islands. For further information, write or call:

> Bureau of Apprenticeship and Training
> U.S. Department of Labor
> 200 Constitution Ave, N.W.
> Washington, DC 20210

PHONE: (202) 219-5921
ON THE INTERNET: http://www.doleta.gov/programs/programs.html

Career Information
The Bureau of Labor Statistics has descriptions of working conditions for a wide variety of specific occupational areas. For more information on the Bureau's publications, write to:

> Bureau of Labor Statistics
> Division of Information Services
> 2 Massachusetts Avenue, N.E.
> Room 2860
> Washington, DC 20212

Information specialists provide a variety of services by telephone: (202) 606-5886
To send a question by fax, please call (202) 606-7890.
ON THE INTERNET: http://stats.bls.gov

Unit 1 JOBS IN INFORMATION HANDLING

> Mail Systems Management Association
> 611 Route 46 West
> Hasbrouck Heights, NJ 07604-3185

PHONE: (201) 393-0004
FAX: (201) 393-9340
ON THE INTERNET: http://www.msma.com

> Transportation Communications
> International Union
> 3 Research Place
> Rockville, MD 20850

PHONE: (301) 948-4910
FAX: (301) 948-1369
TCIU TRAINING INSTITUTE: (301) 948-3510

Unit 2 OFFICE SUPPORT JOBS

> Insurance Information Institute
> 110 William Street
> New York, NY 10038

PHONE: (212) 669-9200
ON THE INTERNET: http://www.iii.org/index.html

Alliance of American Insurers
1501 E. Woodfield Road, Suite 400 West
Schaumburg, IL 60173-4980
PHONE: (847) 517-7474
*Ask for information about jobs for claim
representatives.*

Professional Secretaries International
P.O. Box 20404
Kansas City, MO 64195-0404
PHONE: (816) 891-6600
ON THE INTERNET: http://www.gvi.net/psi
*Ask about the Office Proficiency Assessment
and Certification (OPAC) program.*

National Association of Legal
Secretaries (International)
2250 East 73rd Street, Suite 550
Tulsa, OK 74136
ON THE INTERNET: http://www.nals.org
Ask for the following information:
• *becoming certified as an Accredited Legal
Secretary (ALS)*
• *careers for legal secretaries*

Association of Record Managers and
Administrators (ARMA)
4200 Somerset Drive
Suite 215
Prairie Village, KS 66208
PHONE: (800) 422-2762
ON THE INTERNET: http://www.arma.org/hq

The Society for Human Resource
Management (SHRM)
606 North Washington Street
Alexandria, VA 22314-1997
PHONE: (703) 548-3440
FAX: (703) 836-0367
ON THE INTERNET: http://www.shrm.org

Unit 3 JOBS IN CUSTOMER SERVICE

International Customer Service
Association

401 N. Michigan Avenue
Chicago, IL 60611
PHONE: (800) 360-ICSA (4272)
FAX: (312) 245-1084
EMAIL: icsa@sba.com
ON THE INTERNET: http://www.icsa.com

Reference books:
Ettinger, Blanche; Opportunities in
Customer Service Careers. Lincolnwood,
IL; VGM Career Horizons, 1992.

Martin, William B.; Quality Customer
Service. Menlo Park, CA.; Crisp
Publications, 1993.

Anderson, Kristin; Great Customer
Service on the Telephone. New York, NY;
AMACOM, American Management
Association, 1992.

Blanding, Warren; Customer service
Operations: The Complete Guide.
New York, NY; AMACOM, 1991.

Finch, Lloyd C.; Twenty Ways to
Improve Customer Service. Menlo Park,
CA; Crisp Publications, 1994.

Willingham, Ron; Hey, I'm the
Customer: Front Line Tips for Providing
Superior Customer Service. Englewood
Cliffs, NJ; Prentice Hall, 1992.

Christopher, Martin; The Customer
Service Planner. Oxford, Boston;
Butterworth-Heinemann, 1993.

Broydrick, Stephen C.; How May I Help
You?: Providing Personal Service in an
Impersonal World. Burr Ridge, IL; Irwin
Professional Pub., 1994.

Unit 4 JOBS IN FINANCE

National Association of Credit Management (NACM)
8815 Centre Park Drive
Suite 200
Columbia, Maryland 21045
PHONE: (410) 740-5560
FAX: (410) 740-5574
ON THE INTERNET: http://www.nacm.org
Ask for information about credit education courses.

American Bankers Association
1120 Connecticut Avenue, NW
Washington, DC 20036
PHONE: (800) 338-0626
ON THE INTERNET: http://www.aba.com

American Institute of Banking
An educational service of the American Bankers Association
1120 Connecticut Avenue, NW
Washington, DC 20036
PHONE: (202) 663-5153
ON THE INTERNET: http://www.aba.com/aib.htm

Institute of Financial Education
55 West Monroe Street
Suite 2800
Chicago, IL 60603-5014
PHONE: (800) 946-0488 or (312) 364-0100
ON THE INTERNET:
http://www.theinstitute.com
Ask about training courses for bank workers.

GLOSSARY

access to find, as in to access information on a computer

addressee person to whom mail is sent

applicant person who applies for something, such as a job

authorized given the right and power to do something

authorizers credit workers who approve giving credit to people

balance amount of money that is left in a bank account

clients customers; people who do business with a company

co-applicant person who will share the account

collisions accidents in which two or more cars slide into each other

communicate to share ideas or information with other people

compass rose a map symbol that shows direction

conditions state in which a thing is

convenience ease of use; something that makes a task less difficult

correspondence letters written or received

courteous helpful and polite toward others

coverage losses that an insurance company will pay for

credit amount that is subtracted from the amount that a customer owes

dependents people who depend, or rely on, others to pay for their living expenses, such as children or adults who do not work

destination place that one is going to; address one wishes to reach

dictation material that is read aloud or recorded for a secretary so that he or she can type it

discount lower price

documents papers that contain important information; often legal information

employees people who work for a company or business

exceeds goes beyond

expiration date the date after which something can no longer be used

express special service that is faster than normal

faxes written materials that are sent and received by machines over phone lines

finance charges fees that are charged when customers do not pay their bills in full by the due date

financial having to do with money

firm a business partnership of two or more people

grace period a period of time during which customers do not receive finance charges for money owed

Human Resources Department part of a company that sets rules for hiring and firing, keeps personnel records, and is in charge of training and benefits such as health insurance

insure to protect against loss

interchange the point at which drivers exit a highway or change from one highway to another

interest charges on a loan for the use of the bank's money; also, money that a bank pays savers for the use of their money

interstate between two or more states

invoice detailed list of products and services that were purchased and their costs

job application form that a person fills out when looking for a job at a company

landlord person who owns and rents out apartments or homes to others

legend a list of symbols on a map and their meanings

lines of credit money available to borrow, up to a certain limit

merchandise goods that are bought or sold

minimum the smallest amount allowed

net income money earned after expenses are paid

operating expenses the amount it costs a company to run its business

performance reviews ratings of how well or poorly people do their work

posted recorded a payment or a charge

prerequisites courses that must be taken earlier

products things that businesses make to sell

punctuality being on time

purchase order code a business uses to classify its own orders

quality excellence

quantity amount

recommend make a suggestion

reference number a number given to an item to track it from mailing to delivery

references people or businesses in a position to recommend another; statements about a person's dependability

registration enrollment or sign up

remittance payment sent to a business that supplied a product or service

reschedule make another time for an appointment; make another plan

routine maintenance regular work to keep something performing well

satisfaction happiness or contentment with a job well done

services things that businesses do to help customers or other businesses

statement of account a detailed bill that describes transactions that occurred over a period of time

supervisors people who direct the work of others

supplier a company that sells goods that a business needs

surveys a set of questions asking for facts and opinions

term amount of time given to repay a loan

terms the rules or conditions that a customer and a company have agreed upon

transactions business exchanges; for example, providing a product in exchange for money

transfer switch a telephone call from one place to another

unit price one part of the cost; the cost for one piece

update to give the latest news or information about a situation

verify check information to make sure that it is true

vicinity a nearby area or neighborhood

word processing typing and revising on the computer

workers' compensation insurance that pays workers for losses due to job injuries

INDEX

A N S W E R   K E Y

UNIT ONE: JOBS IN INFORMATION HANDLING

Lesson 1: Working as a Receptionist

CHECK YOUR UNDERSTANDING

page 5

1. c
2. a
3. b
4. d
5. Your answer may be something like this: the title helped me find the main idea by telling me the subject of the reading. Knowing the subject gave me a clue to what the reading is about.

CHECK YOUR UNDERSTANDING

page 8

1. d
2. c
3. c
4. a
5. b
6. The main idea of the information sheet from C&D Telephone Systems is that C&D uses a system of codes to organize long-distance service.

LESSON WRAP-UP

page 9

Your answers may be something like these:

1. Finding main ideas will help my reading by making me pay attention to the most important ideas in whatever I am reading.
2. I am an aide at a day-care center. The center serves a large company. The center and the company wrote a manual that helps aides do a good job. I have to understand the main ideas to do my job right. The company and the center expect me to understand the main ideas.

Lesson 2: Handling Mail and Packages

CHECK YOUR UNDERSTANDING

page 13

1. b
2. c
3. a
4. Pamela Harris; Harris and Associates
5. 800 Riverside Drive, Ocean Air, CA 95945
6. Saturday
7. Yes, I would insure the packages. The instruction sheet says that it is best to insure packages worth more than $100.00, and these packages are worth $5,000.00.

CHECK YOUR UNDERSTANDING

page 16

1. SD
2. SD
3. MI
4. SD
5. MI
6. SD
7. SD
8. SD
9. b
10. d

LESSON WRAP-UP

page 17

Your answers may be something like these:

1. Finding the supporting details will help my reading because I have to find recipes for foods that my husband can eat. I am always looking for details about the amount of fat and salt in foods.
2. Once I worked as an aide in a company health office. I had to read the lists of medicines we kept in the office. When they were sent to us, I read the details of what had arrived. I needed to know details such as expiration dates, proper storage, etc.

Lesson 3: Delivering Messages By Hand

CHECK YOUR UNDERSTANDING

page 21

  1.c

  2.a

  3.b

  4.b

  5.c

  6.a

CHECK YOUR UNDERSTANDING

page 24

  1.d

  2.b

  3.a

  4.d

  5.a

LESSON WRAP-UP

page 25

Your answers may be something like these:

  1.Following directions will help my reading because I read a lot of recipes. To have the food turn out right, I have to follow directions. I need to know what to mix together and in what order. I also need to know how long to cook foods.

  2.I worked as a cook in a fast-food restaurant. I read recipes all the time. I had to follow directions to get the amounts right. If I made too much, I wasted food and money. If I made too little, we ran out of food to sell.

UNIT ONE REVIEW

page 26

Your answers may be something like these:

  1.To find the main idea of a paragraph, look for an idea that sums up the most important point being made in the paragraph.

  2.It is important to find supporting details when you read at work. Details help you understand and remember more of what you read. Knowing more about what you read will help you do a better job.

  3.Following directions can be an important skill in the workplace because you may have to do things in a certain order. The directions could tell you how to do a task step by step.

  4.I would be interested in working as a receptionist at a busy company. I would enjoy learning how the phone system works. I also would enjoy meeting people. I could find out more about this job by looking through want ads for receptionists to see what skills are needed. It would be important to have good reading skills for this job because I would have to read manuals to understand the phone system. I would also have to read instructions from my employer.

UNIT TWO: OFFICE SUPPORT JOBS

Lesson 4: Working as a Secretary

CHECK YOUR UNDERSTANDING

page 31

  1.c

  2.b

  3.d

  4.a

  5.c

CHECK YOUR UNDERSTANDING

page 34

  1.a

  2.c

  3.b

  4.d

  5.Your answer may be something like this: D&K Floor Repair could make sure it doesn't schedule work unless it has enough of the correct finish to complete the job.

LESSON WRAP-UP

page 35

Your answers may be something like these:

  1.Making inferences will help my reading by giving me the skills to read "between the lines." Even if something isn't directly stated, I will be able to figure out the meaning.

  2.I have a job as an aide in a classroom. Sometimes, I read the children's stories and look at their pictures. Often, the stories are about the children and their families. When a child is upset, I can sometimes read between the lines of his or her story to figure out what is bothering the child.

Lesson 5: Working in Personnel

CHECK YOUR UNDERSTANDING

page 39

1. d
2. c
3. a
4. b
5. d

6. Your answer may be something like this: SFTY 100 is a course for supervisors. The title explains that the supervisors will be taught how to watch for problems. They will be learning how to make sure their employees work safely. SFTY 102 also covers basic safety rules, but it is for employees. The people in this course will be learning how to apply the safety rules in their own jobs.

CHECK YOUR UNDERSTANDING

page 42

1. c
2. b
3. a
4. d
5. a

6. Your answer may be something like these: I would hire Stuart Lee because he gets a lot of work done each day. He uses his time well and meets department goals. Or, I would hire Annie Kim because she used her time well and is able to meet the department goals in terms of quantity of work completed, seldom making any errors. Also, it is rare that she is absent or late for work.

LESSON WRAP-UP

page 43

Your answers may be something like these:
1. Being able to compare and contrast

will help my reading by giving me the skill to see what is the same and different about two things. That helps me make choices that are better for me.

2. I am a clerk in a food market. I work in the produce department, where we sell fruits and vegetables. Each day, we get foods from all over the world. I have to read to contrast where they came from. For example, we get oranges from South America and from Florida. By contrasting where the oranges come from and comparing the prices, I know how much to charge for them.

Lesson 6: Checking Insurance Forms

CHECK YOUR UNDERSTANDING

page 47

1. c
2. a
3. d

4. Here is a sample answer: Insurance companies may set limits on how much they will cover so that repairs will be made in a timely way. They would also like to stop people and businesses from making unfair or false claims. Otherwise, insurance companies would lose money and go out of business.

CHECK YOUR UNDERSTANDING

page 50

1. b
2. c
3. b
4. d

5. Your answer may be something like this: You can conclude that the injury to the employee's leg has not healed. The injury may prevent him from driving and from making deliveries.

LESSON WRAP-UP

page 51

Your answers may be something like these:
1. Drawing conclusions as I read will help my understanding because I will recall what I already know and how it fits

in with what I am reading. By thinking about "old" and "new" facts, I can make better decisions.

2. I was a stock assistant in a pharmacy. Sometimes, I had to read information to find out facts about new medicines. Then, I had to think about what I already knew about storing medicines and how they are grouped together. By drawing conclusions as I read, I was better able to figure out where the new items should be placed in the store.

UNIT TWO REVIEW
page 52

Your answers may be something like these:

1. Making inferences is looking at clues to figure something out that is not stated directly. You use clues from the main idea and supporting details. For example, if I read that someone enjoyed working on a project with me, I could infer that they would like to work with me again.

2. When you compare the details in a reading, you are looking to see how the details are alike. When you contrast the details, you are looking to see how the details are different.

3. Keep in mind what you know about the job when looking at the job applications. Try to match the skills needed on the job with the information about people's past jobs and tasks. Draw your conclusion about who would be best for the job based on that information.

4. I would be interested in working as an insurance processing clerk. I like helping people and working with details. To learn more about the job, I could talk to someone in the health insurance department at work. I could ask one of the workers to let me see some of the forms they use. Reading is an important skill in this job because there are many details to take care of. There are also many instructions that must be followed.

UNIT THREE: JOBS IN CUSTOMER SERVICE

Lesson 7: Taking Customers' Orders

CHECK YOUR UNDERSTANDING

page 57

1. b
2. c
3. a
4. a
5. The order clerk will call the customer. Step 1 of the order form has information that the clerk needs. The clerk will get the customer's telephone number from the "Bill to" section of the order form.
6. It would cost $7.98 to send the clothes. The order clerk would read "Shipping and Handling Charges" in Step 3 of the order form.

CHECK YOUR UNDERSTANDING

page 60

1. b
2. c
3. a
4. d
5. Your answer may be something like this: The account number or business telephone number could be helpful. Also, if the order clerk were using a computer, the clerk could search for the order using the name of the company, the name of the person placing the order, or even the zip code in the address. Purchase order numbers come from the customers. It's possible for two customers to send purchase orders with the same number. The order clerk would probably not use the purchase order number to search for an order.

LESSON WRAP-UP

page 61

Your answers may be something like these:

1. Being able to classify information will help my reading because I will know how to put information in common groups. This will help me sort and organize the

information. Classifying information will also help me find things that have already been classified.

2. I work in a fruit and vegetable market. The prices of the foods depend on what group they are in: 1) grown in the area, 2) grown somewhere else in the country, 3) grown in another country, and 4) grown with or without chemicals. I have to read to find out how to group and price each food.

Lesson 8: Working in an Auto Club
CHECK YOUR UNDERSTANDING
page 65
1. d
2. a
3. c
4. c
5. c
6. a

CHECK YOUR UNDERSTANDING
page 68
1. b
2. d
3. c
4. c
5. Your answer may be something like this: Take Route 95 north to the interchange with Route 10. Drive west on Route 10 to the interchange with Route 75. Drive north on Route 75 to Valdosta.

LESSON WRAP-UP
page 69
Your answers may be something like these:
1. At home, while watching the news, people read weather maps. These maps show wind direction. In school, people read world maps. These maps show main parts of the world, like Europe, Asia, Africa, and the Americas. People who work for the post office read route maps. These maps show which blocks are on each mail deliverer's route.
2. People might need to read maps to plan a road trip. People might also read

maps to figure out what bus to take to work. Finally, people might read maps to find stores in a shopping center or a mall.

3. The city that I live in has many places of interest to children. I want to take my children to the zoo, to the Children's Museum, and to the Children's Library. Knowing how to read road maps will help me find the best way to get to each of these places.

Lesson 9: Meeting Customers' Needs
CHECK YOUR UNDERSTANDING
page 73
1. a
2. d
3. c
4. b
5. d

CHECK YOUR UNDERSTANDING
page 76
1. d
2. b
3. c
4. a

LESSON WRAP-UP
page 77
Your answers may be something like these:
1. Being able to distinguish fact from opinion will help my reading because I will be able to make up my own mind about things. I don't have to accept what others say as true. They may be giving an opinion, and I have to recognize that.
2. I work in a school cafeteria. Sometimes, we survey the children and the teachers about the food. Some of the answers are facts. Others are opinions. I have to be able to distinguish between the two to know what decisions to make.

UNIT THREE REVIEW
page 78
Your answers may be something like these:
1. Grouping similar facts together can help you organize your thinking. Being

able to classify information can also make it easier to find what you are looking for. You can figure out in which part of a file or form you should look.

2. I would use this strategy for reading a map: First, I would find the compass rose to see which way north is on the map. Second, I would read the legend and look for any familiar names or landmarks. Third, I would find the place that I am now and the place that I need to go. Finally, I would plan a way to get to where I needed to go.

3. A fact is true. It can be checked or tested. An opinion is a belief. There is usually not any way to prove that an opinion is true.

4. I would like to work as a customer service representative. I like to solve problems and work with people. I could learn more about this kind of work by talking to people in the customer service department of a store. Good reading skills are important in this job because you have to follow written rules when solving customers' problems.

UNIT FOUR: JOBS IN FINANCE

Lesson 10: Working as a Bank Teller

CHECK YOUR UNDERSTANDING

page 83
1. c
2. d
3. b
4. a
5. c

CHECK YOUR UNDERSTANDING

page 86
1. d
2. b
3. a
4. c
5. b

LESSON WRAP-UP

page 87

Your answers may be something like these:

1. Identifying the cause and effect in reading material will help my reading because I have children who often need medicine. This skill helps me to read the labels on their medicines. I need to be able to think about the effect I want, and then do the right thing to cause that effect.

2. I was an aide in a school office. I read notes from parents about their children. Sometimes, the notes were about not letting the children exercise or eat a certain food. I needed to identify the causes and their effects. Otherwise, the children might have become ill.

Lesson 11: Checking Credit Information

CHECK YOUR UNDERSTANDING

page 91
1. b
2. c
3. d
4. b
5. Your answer may be something like this: Yes, the credit clerk needs to call the applicant. She asked for a joint account but did not fill out the information about the other person who would use the credit card.

CHECK YOUR UNDERSTANDING

page 94
1. a
2. c
3. d
4. d
5. b

LESSON WRAP-UP

page 95

Your answers may be something like these:

1. Being able to draw conclusions from what I read will help me by allowing me to make good decisions. When I look through

ANSWER KEY

want ads, I have to draw conclusions about whether a job seems right for me.

2. I was a cashier in a restaurant. Part of my job was to look at the bill when it was being paid. I would check for errors. I learned to draw conclusions about the numbers. Sometimes, I would look at a total and know it couldn't be enough. By quickly looking at prices, my conclusion was that the total was wrong. When this happened, I always added up the bill again.

Lesson 12: Preparing Bills

CHECK YOUR UNDERSTANDING
page 99

1. a
2. d
3. c
4. b
5. b
6. Your answer may be something like this: The details give the customer a record of what he or she bought, what payments were made, and how much is owed. This information can help the customer find mistakes in billing. If the statement just listed an amount owed, the customer would have a hard time telling if the bill was correct.

CHECK YOUR UNDERSTANDING
page 102

1. c
2. a
3. c
4. b
5. Your answer may be something like this: The customer's account is being charged a 2% finance charge. In 10 more days, the bill will reach 90 days without payment. The account will then be charged a 5% finance charge. Also, the customer will have to pay for any future office visits in full at the time of service.

LESSON WRAP-UP
page 103

Your answers may be something like these:

1. Finding supporting details will improve my reading by helping me understand what I need to do. My on-the-job reading is based on lists of details. I have to put together items in a certain order.
2. I clean business offices at night. Sometimes, my supervisor leaves a list of tasks for me to do that are different from my everyday tasks. I need to understand the details on the list so that I can get the job done right.

UNIT FOUR REVIEW
page 104

Your answers may be something like these:

1. A cause is an action that makes something happen. The effect is the thing that happens.
2. It takes me about 10 minutes to get to class from my home. One time, I left my home at 6:20 to go to class. When I got to class, the clock on the wall said it was 6:15. I concluded that the clock in the class was slow.
3. The supporting details are important because they tell more about the main idea. They can add to your understanding of the main idea.
4. I would like to be a bank teller. I enjoy working with money. I would also like the different tasks a bank teller has to do. To learn more about the job, I could visit a bank near my home. I could talk to the head teller about what skills a good bank teller should have. Bank tellers would need to read the bank account slips, the steps for handling money, and the information on forms.